KOREAN WAR
ALLIED SURGE

PYONGYANG FALLS, UN SWEEP TO THE YALU OCTOBER 1950

GERRY VAN TONDER

Pen & Sword
MILITARY

AN IMPRINT OF PEN & SWORD BOOKS LTD.
YORKSHIRE – PHILADELPHIA

First published in Great Britain in 2019 by
PEN AND SWORD MILITARY
an imprint of
Pen and Sword Books Ltd
47 Church Street
Barnsley
South Yorkshire S70 2AS

Copyright © Gerry van Tonder, 2019

ISBN 978 1 52675 692 3

Typeset by Aura Technology and Software Services, India
Maps, drawings and militaria in the colour section by Colonel Dudley Wall
Printed and bound by TJ International Ltd, Padstow, Cornwall

Pen & Sword Books Ltd incorporates the imprints of Pen & Sword
Archaeology, Atlas, Aviation, Battleground, Discovery, Family History, History, Maritime, Military,
Naval, Politics, Railways, Select, Social History, Transport, True Crime, Claymore Press, Frontline
Books, Leo Cooper, Praetorian Press, Remember When, Seaforth Publishing and Wharncliffe.

For a complete list of Pen and Sword titles please contact
Pen and Sword Books Limited
47 Church Street, Barnsley, South Yorkshire, S70 2AS, England
email: enquiries@pen-and-sword.co.uk
website: www.pen-and-sword.co.uk

or
Pen and Sword Books
1950 Lawrence Rd, Havertown, PA 19083, USA
email: uspen-and-sword@casematepublishers.com
www.penandswordbooks.com

CONTENTS

GLOSSARY

APC	armour-piercing, capped
Bn	battalion
CCF	Chinese Communist Forces
CIA	Central Intelligence Agency (US)
DPRK	Democratic People's Republic of Korea (North Korea)
EUSAK	Eighth United States Army in Korea
FAB	field artillery battalion
FEAF	Far East Air Forces (US)
HE	high explosive
HVAP	high-velocity armour-piercing
JOC	Joint Operations Centre
JCS	Joint Chiefs of Staff (US)
KATUSA	Korean Augmentation to the US Army
KMAG	Korea Military Advisory Group (US)
KPA	Korean People's Army (North Korean)
LCVP	landing craft, vehicle, personnel
LSM (R)	landing ship, rocket
LST	landing ship, tank
LVT	landing vehicle, tracked
MASH	Mobile Army Surgical Hospital
MLR	main line of resistance
MSR	main supply route
NSC	National Security Council
PRC	People's Republic of China
RCT	Regimental Combat Team
ROK	Republic of Korea (South Korea)
ROKA	Republic of Korea Army (South Korean)
TACP	Tactical Air Control Party
TF	task force
UN	United Nations
UNC	United Nations Command
UNTCOK	United Nations Temporary Commission on Korea
USAFIK	US Army Forces in Korea
USMC	United States Marine Corps

It will be noticed that many Korean names of places and geographical features either carry the same suffix or end in the same few letters. These define what a name is being applied to, e.g. Ch'ŏng*ch'ŏn* is Ch'ŏng River:

ch'ŏn / gang	river
do	island
dong	town or village within a district (*ri*)
ni	town
ri	town and surrounding district
san	mountain

The first South African Air Force (SAAF) contingent to arrive for duty in Korea on parade upon arrival at Johnson Air Base, Japan in October 1950. (Syd de la Harpe)

TIMELINE

1945

August: Japan surrenders and US President Harry S. Truman signs the instrument allowing for the temporary divide of the Korean peninsula at the 38th Parallel: Soviet forces to the north and American forces the south.

1946

February: Kim Il-sung is appointed to the head of a Marxist-Leninist provisional government in the Soviet zone: the People's Committee of North Korea.

1947

November: Despite Soviet opposition, the UN accepts a US-endorsed plan for global elections in Korea to vote for a single government.

1948

May: Elections are held, but only in South Korea.

July: The North Korean People's Congress draws up its own constitution.

September: The Democratic People's Republic of Korea (DPRK) is proclaimed, with Kim Il-sung as the first North Korean leader; Moscow withdraws its troops from North Korea.

1949

June: The last US combat forces leave South Korea.

1950

25 June: Massed North Korean troops, armour and artillery cross the 38th Parallel, invading South Korea.

28 June: The Korean People's Army (KPA) capture the South Korean capital, Seoul.

8 July: US President Truman appoints General Douglas MacArthur to head United Nations Command (UNC) forces.

10 July: The US 25th Infantry Division starts arriving in Korea from Japan.

12 July: Lieutenant General Walton H. Walker, commander of the US Eighth Army, is placed in command of UNC ground troops.

18 July: The US 1st Cavalry Division starts arriving in Korea.

29 July: The US 2nd Infantry Division starts arriving in Korea.

2 August: The US 1st Provisional Marine Brigade arrives in Korea; US I Corps is mobilized at Fort Bragg in readiness for deployment to Korea.

4 August: UNC forces dig in along the Naktong River, in what becomes known as the Pusan Perimeter.

15 September: Spearheaded by the US Marines, the US X Corps lands at Inch'ŏn on the Korean west coast, to the rear of North Korean occupation forces.

16 September: The US Eighth Army commences its breakout from the Pusan Perimeter.

23 September: North Korean forces begin a general withdrawal from the Pusan Perimeter front; US IX Corps becomes operational at Miryang.

27 September: UNC forces liberate Seoul.

1 October: South Korean President Syngman Rhee orders his troops across the 38th Parallel.

3 October: Communist China warns it will cross its border with North Korea to defend that nation should non-Korean forces cross the 38th Parallel.

7 October: The United Nations overwhelmingly passes a resolution authorizing UN forces to cross the 38th Parallel.

14 October: Chinese Communist Forces (CCF) commence crossing into North Korea from Manchuria.

15 October: General MacArthur and US President Truman meet, for the first time, on Wake Island; CCF anti-aircraft fire brings down a US F-51 Mustang Fighter, the first such event of the conflict.

19 October: UN forces enter the North Korean capital, P'yŏngyang.

20 October: More than 2,800 troops and 300 tons of matériel of the US 187th Airborne Regimental Combat Team are dropped by parachute at Sukch'ŏn and Sunch'ŏn, north of P'yŏngyang.

24 October: General MacArthur authorizes his troops to move all the way to the Chinese border at the Yalu River.

25 October: All restrictions are lifted on UN close-air support missions near the Yalu River.

26 October: South Korean troops reach the Yalu River at Ch'ŏsan; Chinese forces maul a South Korean battalion near Onjŏng.

27 October: The South Korean 6th Infantry Division is attacked by elements of the CCF near the Yalu River.

29 October: US Far East Air Forces (FEAF) C-47 Skytrain aircraft conduct medical evacuation and supply missions from Sinanju, 40 miles north of P'yŏngyang, the airfield the farthest north from which FEAF would operate during the war.

INTRODUCTION

On 2 September 1945, on the deck of the USS *Missouri*, at anchor in Tokyo Bay, US General of the Army and Supreme Commander for the Allied Powers, Douglas MacArthur, formally accepted the Japanese instruments of surrender, ending the Second World War. In compliance with the provisions of the historic document, Chief of Staff of the US Army, Lieutenant General Richard K. Sutherland, issued 'General Order No. 1, Military and Naval', ordering, inter alia:

> The senior Japanese Commanders and all ground, sea, air and auxiliary forces within Korea North of 38 degrees North latitude ... shall surrender to the Commander-in-Chief of Soviet Forces in the Far East ... and Korea South of 38 degrees North latitude shall surrender to the Commander-in-Chief, U. S. Army Forces, Pacific.

Six weeks earlier, socialist Clement Attlee had replaced Britain's cigar-toting, war-time icon Winston Churchill at Downing Street. Social imperatives in his war-devastated nation demanded Atlee's full attention, so the interim division and political future of a distant Asian peninsula held little interest.

After only four months in the White House, US President Harry S. Truman had, in his own words, the 'fateful responsibility' of bringing Armageddon to the Japanese cities of Hiroshima and Nagasaki. The Japanese empire collapsed immediately, and with it the demise of its thirty-five-year hegemonic occupancy of the Korean peninsula.

Like their allies in London, Washington did not regard Korea as falling within the American Far East sphere of influence, consequently terminating its military caretaking role south of the 38th Parallel after elections in 1948 that saw the establishment of a South Korean government under Syngman Rhee. As the Americans left for home, they left a pro-Western nation totally impoverished of any semblance of self-defence capabilities.

In Soviet Russia, the only Allied-conference constant, Joseph Stalin, had been catapulted into demagogue status as a 'Defender of the Fatherland'. Reputed to have said that he trusted no one, including himself, the dictator would not turn his back on that part of Korea north of the 38th. In P'yŏngyang, Stalin discovered and nurtured a North Korean protégé to do his proxy bidding on the Korean peninsula. Kim Il-sung, the father of North Korea's ruling dynasty, became the privileged recipient of a staggering array of military arms and equipment, supplemented with hundreds of top Soviet advisors. However, seated firmly in the Kremlin's benevolence were Stalin's designs of regional expansionism. The CIA referred to the concept of 'unfriendly control'.

In the secret weekly intelligence highlights for the week 5 to 11 April 1950, the CIA's Far East/Pacific Division reported that the North Korean air force, comprising thirty-six 'obsolescent World War II fighters' and with its 'Soviet-trained personnel … possesses complete air superiority over the South Korean air force, which has no combat aircraft'. Although regarded as small, it was believed that the North Korean air regiment would be able to provide material air support to ground forces in any attempted invasion of the south.

Of far greater concern, expressed in the same report, however, was a predicted imminent amphibious attack by Chinese Communist forces on the Chou Shan (Zhoushan) archipelago, only 350 miles from Nationalist Taiwan. Some 355,000 troops of General Chen Yi's Third Field Army, with air support from the 'Soviet-assisted Communist air force' would target the capture of forward naval and military bases from which a major assault would be launched against the island of Taiwan.

At 3 p.m. on Saturday, 24 June 1950, as summer temperatures soared into the thirties, the US government machinery in Washington was in holiday mode: President Truman was on his way to his private residence in Independence, Missouri, Army Chief of Staff, General Joseph 'Lightning Joe' Collins was basking on a beach on the Chesapeake, and Secretary of State Dean Acheson was enjoying a break at Harewood Farm in Maryland. Thirteen hours ahead, at 4 a.m. on Sunday 25 June, North Korean People's Army (KPA) commander, General Choi Yung Kun, received the green light from Kim Il-sung to launch 95,000 troops from seven infantry divisions and one armoured division across the 38th Parallel into South Korea.

In the first in a series of titles on battles of the Korean War, *North Korea Invades the South: Across the 38th Parallel, June 1950*,* the author looks at the surprise attack that caught the Americans totally unprepared. The combined US and Republic of Korea Army (ROKA) forces were helpless against the communist onslaught that was spearheaded by Russian-built T-34/85 tanks. In many instances, disorderly flight—including open desertion—rather than tactical withdrawals characterized the rout.

By mid-July, the North Koreans had trapped the US Eighth Army and ROKA forces, the latter under their Chief of Staff Lieutenant General Chung Il-kwon, on the south-eastern tip of the Korean peninsula, in a fiercely defended enclave known as the Pusan Perimeter. In his second title on battles of the Korean War, *North Korean Onslaught: UN Stand at the Pusan Perimeter, August–September 1950*,† the author follows the desperate mobile defence tactics of overall commander Lieutenant General Walton Walker in a series of hard-fought battles to prevent his forces from being pushed into the Sea of Japan.

In Tokyo, the controversial, impulsive career soldier and lauded Second World War veteran, General Douglas MacArthur, sought to exploit General Walker's successful stand on the Pusan Perimeter. Against all odds, on 15 September 1950, the US X Corps executed a daring amphibious assault on the west coast Korean port of Inch'ŏn. In the ensuing

---

* Pen and Sword Books, Barnsley, 2018.

† Ibid.

US Marines come ashore at Inchon in an amphibious tractor. (Photo USMC)

days following the establishing of four beachheads, MacArthur fulfilled his master plan of enveloping the entire North Korean invasion force, with General Walker breaking out of the Pusan Perimeter from the south. The author gives a full account of the campaign in his third title on battles of the Korean War, *Inchon Landing: MacArthur's Korean War Masterstroke, September 1950.*[*]

---

[*] Ibid.

The South Korean capital, Seoul, had been liberated and President Rhee returned to the seat of government. But for General MacArthur, who only weeks earlier had endorsed the tactical use of nuclear warheads against the enemy, there could only be one logical outcome: the total emasculation of North Korea's military machine. While his UN forces were poised to cross the 38th Parallel in hot pursuit of the routed North Korean army, in Washington politicians, intelligence services and military supremoes were forced to contemplate the regional ramifications of a military invasion into the Democratic People's Republic of Korea (DPRK).

In a top secret paper, 'Study of CIA Reporting on Chinese Communist Intervention in the Korean War, September 1950', released by CIA Historical Staff on 17 October 1955, an indictment was levelled of 'misrepresentations' against intelligence and estimates reports of the time:

> The principal reason for these misrepresentations was a failure to gauge Chinese Communist and, more particularly, Soviet strategy with respect to the Korean War accurately in the context of the world situation.
>
> Although those responsible for United States strategy in the Korean War during September to December 1950 were made fully aware by CIA that Communist China represented a grave potential danger to the UN cause, the tenor of CIA reporting was such as to suggest that the danger would not materialize.
>
> When Chinese/Soviet forces did not intervene (a) at Inchon (September 15); (b) at the crossing of the 38th Parallel (October 7); or (c) at the moment when UN forces reached the Yalu (November 1), CIA appeared to adopt the assumption that they would not do so at all.

On 9 September 1950, the US National Security Council (NSC) submitted to the White House its report NSC 81/1 for presidential approval and 'implementation by all executive departments and agencies of the U.S. Government'.*

In essence, the NSC, quoting United Nations resolutions in 1947, 1948, 1949 and 1950, fully endorsed the international body's objective of complete independence and unity of Korea. Without 'substantially increasing the risk of general war with the Soviet Union or Communist China', the NSC stressed that it would be in the national interest to 'advocate the pressing of the United Nations action to this conclusion'.

> As U.N. forces succeed in stabilizing the front, driving back the North Korean forces, and approaching the 38th Parallel, the decisions and actions taken by the United States and other U.N. members which are supporting the Security Council

---

* 'United States Courses of Action with Respect to Korea', 9 September 1950, History and Public Policy Program Digital Archive, Truman Presidential Museum and Library

resolutions, and those taken by the Kremlin, will determine whether hostilities are confined to operations against the North Koreans or spread so that the danger of a third world war is greatly increased.

The report added that there was a 'clear legal basis for taking such military actions north of the 38th parallel as are necessary in accomplishing this mission'. However, the NSC strongly emphasized that the crossing of the 38th, with the possibility of occupying North Korea, would require approval by UN member states. Finally, with the neutralization of North Korean forces as a military threat, 'non-Korean forces [including those of the US] should be removed as soon as practicable'.

On 1 October, frustrated by a lack of progress in the UN General Assembly to approve a road map for Korea's future, South Korean President Syngman Rhee ordered his troops into North Korea.

Late on Saturday, 7 October, the General Assembly passed an 'Eight-Power' resolution, giving MacArthur the mandate to cross the 38th Parallel. Forty-seven member states voted in favour of the resolution, while five—the Soviet Union and its supporters—voted against. Eight nations abstained.

Two days later, MacArthur ordered US I Corps in the west and US X Corps in the east to force the 38th. Typically, the UNC commander's commitment was absolute, but the high-risk imponderables were also many, not least of all how Moscow and Beijing might react.

South Korean troops prepare to move. (Photo US Army Korea)

1. MACARTHUR'S RUBICON

'There was at this fateful hour a feeling of elation and of high and successful purpose which the United Nations experienced only rarely.'

UN Secretary General Trygve Lie on the Korean War, early October 1950[*]

As September 1950 drew to a close, United Nations Command (UNC) forces, mostly comprised of American and South Korean troops, consolidated their dispositions along the full west–east axis of the 38th Parallel. UNC supremo General Douglas MacArthur believed that UN Security Council Resolution 83 of 27 June 1950 provided him with the mandate to restore international peace and security on the Korean peninsula by military means, which included the pursuit of the broken North Korean army north of the 38th.

Washington, however, insisted on seeking UN authority to legitimize any military incursions into North Korea, especially with the ever-present threat of Chinese or Soviet intervention in the war. But at Lake Success, the UN General Assembly's temporary headquarters on New York's Long Island, the Soviet delegation caused mayhem in the chamber by insisting that debate about political persecution in Greece had to take priority over the Korean crisis.

In Seoul, South Korean head of state, Syngman Rhee, ran out of patience. On 1 October, he ordered his troops to cross the 38th.

While MacArthur appealed directly to the North Koreans to surrender to avoid 'the early and total defeat and complete destruction of your armed forces and war-making potential', Chinese Premier and Foreign Minister Zhou Enlai was unequivocal in divulging the mood in Beijing. The Soviet TASS News Agency quoted the veteran Chinese doyen of international diplomacy, speaking at a formal function in Beijing to celebrate the first anniversary of the establishment of the establishment of the Chinese People's Republic, as saying that China 'will not stand aside should the Imperialists wantonly invade the territory of its neighbour [North Korea]'.

In a CIA confidential information report of 17 October, it was stated that the Central Committee of the Chinese Communist Party had predicted a long war in Korea 'from which the Americans would not be able to extricate themselves'. The North Korean Army was undefeated and remained a large, powerful force united behind leader Kim Il-sung. The Beijing document added that American Far East forces were now fully committed,

---

[*] Trygve Lie, *In the Cause of Peace: Seven Years with the United Nations* (Macmillan Co., New York, 1954).

WHAT NOW IN KOREA?

This morning's news of the 'closing of the gap' by the two main thrusting branches of the United Nations forces in Korea is as pregnant with interest as it is gratifying. Appreciation of General MacArthur's strategy, which showed nice timing in his tactical withdrawals to the last safe limits while his counterattacks, on land and sea were being mounted, is now supplanted by admiration for the drive shown by the troops under his command.

These successes, it will readily be recognised, must beget serious and immediate problems to which it may be hoped earnest attention has already been given. Seoul is only 40 air miles (and the road, as it happens, is fairly straight) from the 38th Parallel, and the United Nations' troops may well reach that crucial boundary within a matter of days. Where do they go from there?

It is devoutly to be hoped that they will stop just where they are!

The reactions of Soviet Russia, not to mention Communist China, have not been announced, but they can be reasonably foreseen and they might set the world ablaze. Moreover, by crossing the line the United Nations, who so far have unquestionably been repelling an invader and resisting aggression, would almost certainly lose that moral support which at present they quite properly command among all the truly democratic nations. The boot would be on the other foot with vengeance.

President Truman's attitude to this has fortunately already been made clear. He regards the American troops and their commander in Korea as United Nations forces, and will leave it to the United Nations to decide their next move.

Western Daily Press, 27 September 1950

and that 'neither the United States nor other United Nations countries involved in the war can send more troops to Korea; defeat is therefore inevitable'.

The CIA also estimated that, at the time, there were 39,500 ethnic Chinese resident throughout North Korea's eight provinces, engaged primarily in vegetable production, operating restaurants and bakeries, trading and manual labour.

In late 1949, the Communist Chinese had established a military mission in the former Japanese Yi Pyong-hun Hospital in the North Korean capital P'yŏngyang. From early 1950, the mission adopted more of an embassy function, not only to effectively control the Chinese nationals in the city, but also a venue for what remained clandestine meetings with North Korean civilian and military leaders. Radio equipment was also installed to maintain close and regular communications with China.

An 8-inch howitzer of B Battery, 720th FAB, US X Corps, Korea. (Photo US Army)

At the Manchurian city of An-Tung (Dandong), facing Sinŭiju in North Korea across the Sino–Korean Friendship Bridge over the Yalu River, American intelligence revealed that elements of the Chinese People's Volunteer Army (CPVA) XL Corps—commonly referred to as the Mukden Unit—had been assembling. By October, the 354th Regiment of the 118th Infantry Division, CPVA XL Corps, commanded by the 40-year-old Mao Shih-ch'ang, had an estimated strength of 10,000, and was equipped with six 122mm mountain guns and twelve 122mm field pieces. Each battalion was armed with six heavy machine guns and three 120mm mortars, while each company had six light machine guns and three 82mm mortars. Each platoon was equipped with eight Soviet-made rifles and two light machine guns.

Beijing continued to mass her 'volunteer' armies along the Manchurian border with North Korea, such that by the end of October, CPVA Marshal Peng Dehuai would have six armies—eighteen divisions—in the high mountains of central North Korea.

In addition, General Lin Piao's CPVA Fourth Army had returned to Manchuria following the cessation of operations against Hainan and Formosa, bringing the Chinese military strength in Manchuria to an estimated 450,000 by the end of September. At the start of

CHINA'S APPEAL

The Chinese delegate to the United Nations Assembly has spoken movingly on the "grave dangers to world peace and security" in the Far East. There was no need for him to mention Russia by name. But one wonders how many of his audience realise the enormous growth in recent years of Russia's stake in Asia.

This stake directly and indirectly covers everything northwards of a 4,000-mile line from the borders of India to Vladivostok. Outer Mongolia is for practical purposes one of the constituent republics. Sinkiang (or Chinese Turkestan) has for many years been increasingly drawn into the Russian economy and away from China. Northern Korea is a puppet of Moscow's, openly threatening the independence of the Republic in the South. Saghalien and the Kuriles, reaching down to Japan, are all Russia's; and she now has stranglehold on Manchuria, which she has coveted for 50 years.

It is easier to see what has happened than what can now be done, apart from the obvious necessity of concentrating on the restoration of prosperity in other East Asian countries so that they may automatically become bulwarks against Communist expansion. In China nine-tenths of the Communists' success was due to the general detestation of the Kuomintang. Nobody is going to waste equipment on the nationalist troops who obviously will not fight. At present the situation in China is so uncertain that there seems nothing to be done but mark time. One point deserves attention, namely Manchuria, which is particularly dear to Chinese pride. The recovery of all China's sovereign rights first on the Communists' programme; and with the railways and ports in Russia's hands, Manchuria is more Russian than a Chinese possession. There are many who believe that Manchuria will eventually make China, if not less Communist in form, decidedly less pro-Russian in action.

Yorkshire Post and Leeds Intelligencer, 24 September 1949

October, American intelligence reported the presence of a total of thirty-eight Chinese divisions in Manchuria, with sixteen divisions along the Yalu River. However, Washington still maintained that Chinese intervention was improbable, a view that MacArthur subscribed to:

Had they [China] interfered in the first or second months it would have been decisive. We are no longer fearful of their intervention. We no longer stand hat in hand. The Chinese have 300,000 men in Manchuria. Of those probably not more than 100,000 to 125,000 are distributed along the Yalu River. Only 50,000 to

The aftermath of a 356-ton B-29 Superfortress raid on the Northwest P'yŏngyang marshalling yard and repair centre. (Photo NARA)

60,000 could be gotten across the Yalu River. They have no air force. Now that we have bases for our Air Force in Korea, if the Chinese tried to get down to Pyongyang there would be the greatest slaughter.*

In the immediate wake of the UNC counteroffensive at Inch'ŏn, there was considerable North Korean and Soviet activity on the east coast as the US Air Force (USAF) continued with its unrelenting campaign of interdiction bombing. US intelligence reported on Soviet vessels entering Ch'ŏngjin harbour every night to unload vehicles and munitions, while the families of some 200 Soviet advisors were evacuated north from the port city to Najin, 20 miles from the Soviet border and 60 miles from Vladivostok, home of the Soviet Pacific Fleet.

To the south, the area between Ch'ŏngjin and Nanam had been declared a no-go zone to civilians. Around 8,000 North Korean People's Army (KPA) army recruits were undergoing training, while at Nanam airfield US intelligence had reported the presence of twenty-three unidentified fighter aircraft of which twenty sported Soviet markings.

North of Wŏnsan, the east-coast port city of Hŭngnam had been all but totally destroyed by successive FEAF Bomber Command sorties that had started late in July.

On the morning of 30 July, mission 'Nannie Able' saw forty-seven Boeing B-29 Superfortress heavy bombers from squadrons of the USAF 22nd and 92nd

---

* Robert Frank Futrell, *The United States Air Force in Korea, 1950–1953* (Progressive Management, USA, 1983).

bombardment groups conduct an APQ-13-radar raid on the Chosen Nitrogen Explosives Factory in Hŭngnam. Two days later, the same squadrons had carried out a visual bombing raid—'Nannie Baker'—on the adjacent Chosen Nitrogen Fertilizer Factory. The exploding 500-lb. bombs rocked the B-29s at 16,000 feet. On 3 August, thirty-nine B-29s executed 'Nannie Charlie' against a third Hŭngnam strategic target, the Bogun Chemical Plant. Such was the destruction that FEAF commander Lieutenant General George E. Stratemeyer declared that the largest chemical and explosives centre in Asia would 'no longer be considered a major factor in the Korean war.'

In Wŏnsan, railway workshops and an oil refinery were also subjected to FEAF strategic bombing during this period, a certain prerequisite for MacArthur's plans for a North Korean east-coast invasion. Under Major General Emmett O'Donnell, from 13 July to 31 October Bomber Command averaged nine B-29 sorties a month, dropping 30,136 tons of bombs on strategic targets in North Korea.

By mid-September, the KPA headquarters had been translocated from P'yŏngyang south to Ch'ŏrwŏn, around 16 miles from the 38th. Approximately 7,000 KPA troops had been deployed to the vicinity, equipped with a large but undetermined number of

Chosen Oil Refinery at the North Korean east coast port of Wŏnsan, levelled by US Far East Air Forces interdiction bombing. (Photo USAF)

ATROCITIES TO BE INVESTIGATED

U.N. Team for Taejon.

The United Nations have decided to investigate the atrocities alleged to have been committed by Communists at Taejon, and a team has left Taegu for the purpose.

A United Nations team left Taegu to-day for Taejon to investigate atrocities alleged to have been committed by North Koreans just before they evacuated that city. The team went at the request of General Walker, American 8th Army commander.

The number of American prisoners killed by the North Koreans before they fled is now put at about 30 and not 40 as reported earlier; but the number of South Koreans alleged to have been murdered is mounting as new burial places are found. It is now put at nearly 1,000. At one point 400 civilians were lined up before two graves, each 75 yards long, and mown down by machine-guns, anti-Communist sources said. The bodies of 250 people were found in a common grave on hillside near a church. Another 100 bodies, riddled with machine-gun bullets, were discovered jammed in basement, states Reuter.

Nottingham Evening Post, 30 September 1950

anti-aircraft guns and artillery pieces. Twenty large tanks and munitions were known to have been placed in nearby tunnels. Although the KPA headquarters was at Ch'ŏrwŏn, many high-ranking North Korean officers, including Supreme Commander of the KPA, Ch'oe Yong-gŏn, elected instead to establish themselves at Kowŏn, an important KPA supply centre.

In anticipation of a UN counteroffensive from the south, on about 20 September the North Korean authorities ordered the civilian evacuation from P'yŏngyang to Yŏngdŏk and other towns in that area.

On 2 October, the UNC issued an operations plan, in which it appeared that greater consideration had been given for logistics and the North Korean terrain than that for KPA opposition, reflecting a painless expedition across the 38th. MacArthur's intelligence chief, Major General Charles A. Willoughby, described the plan as 'the classical one made by [Prussian Field Marshal] Von Moltke: action by separated forces off the enemy's axis of movement.'*

Essentially, General Walton Walker's US Eighth Army was to strike north overland along the Kaesŏng–Sariwŏn axis to take P'yŏngyang. The US X Corps, under Lieutenant

---

* Ibid.

General Edward M. Almond would effect an amphibious landing at the east-coast port city of Wŏnsan, thereby establishing a line of defence across the Korean peninsula along a Chŏng-ju–Kunmŏ-ri–Yŏngwŏn–Hamhŭng–Hŭngnam axis. Only South Korean troops would have the authority to launch missions north of this line. The manoeuvre would encircle the North Korean troops to allow for maximum neutralization of the enemy threat. There was, however, an element of dissent among some of MacArthur's commanding staff.

Major General David G. Barr, commander of the 7th Infantry Division, US X Corps, preferred an overland move from Seoul to Wŏnsan. Senior USAF officers feared that the Wŏnsan port infrastructure would not cope with the sudden massive influx of personnel and equipment, contending that this would impact negatively on the combat capabilities of both the US Eighth Army and USAF air support. Chief of Staff of Naval Forces Far East would comment years later: 'We objected to Wŏnsan being unnecessary. It took a lot of troops out of action for a long time when the enemy was already on the run. We felt the same objective could be achieved by marching the X Corps up a road leading from Seoul to Wŏnsan.'[*]

General Almond brushed the concerns aside: 'going overland is simply out of the question. Half of our equipment would be left in ditches by the side of the road.'[†] What was as disturbing to many an American officer was MacArthur's insistence that all ground forces would fall under two 'completely self-sustaining' independent commands: Walker's and Almond's.

Not for the first time, and on the premise that he still clutched the UN mandate to combat the North Korean army wherever and whenever, the unmanageable MacArthur issued his own call for the enemy to immediately lay down their arms—the general was in no doubt that the American nation would trust and endorse whatever course of action the mastermind of the Inch'ŏn victory elected to take to end the conflict. There would be no need to consult Washington nor await the outcome of diplomatic niceties at the UN. In a broadcast from Tokyo, MacArthur addressed the Commander-in-Chief of North Korean forces:

Early and total defeat and complete destruction of your armed forces and war-making potential is now inevitable.

In order that the decisions of the United Nations may be carried out with a minimum of further loss of life and destruction of property I, as United Nations Commander-in-Chief, call upon you and the forces under your command—in whatever part of Korea they are situated—forthwith to lay down your arms and cease hostilities under such military supervision as I may direct.

---

* Ibid.

† Ibid.

General MacArthur (centre) with US Eighth Army commander, Lieutenant General Walton Walker (far right).

I shall anticipate your early decision upon this opportunity to avoid further and useless shedding of blood, the destruction of property—Douglas MacArthur.
The Canberra Times, Monday, 2 October 1950

While Washington, Lake Success and MacArthur deliberated in a triangle of divergent interpretations of the international legalities of UNC forces crossing the 38th Parallel, the South Koreans clung on to their president Syngman Rhee's promise in Pusan on 19 September: 'We have to advance as far as the Manchurian border until not a single enemy soldier is left in our country ... we will not allow ourselves to stop.'*

On the afternoon of 29 September, at Kangnŭng on the central east Korean coast, Lieutenant Colonel Rollins S. Emmerich, Korean Military Advisory Group (KMAG) advisor to ROKA I Corps, received orders for the ROKA 3rd Infantry Division to cross the 38th and advance on Wŏnsan. The message was from ROKA Chief of Staff Chŏng Il-kwŏn who, the day before, had secured permission from US Eighth Army CO General Walker for one ROKA company to temporarily operate north of the 38th. The following morning, ROKA reconnaissance patrols crossed the 38th.

---

* Roy E Appleman, 'South to the Naktong, North to the Yalu (June–November 1950)', *United States in the Korean War*. (Center Of Military History, United States Army, Washington, D.C., 1992).

Around midday the next day, 1 October, two ROKA rifle companies also crossed into North Korea, encountering desultory enemy fire from old established outposts.

On 2 October, the 3rd and Capital divisions, ROKA I Corps, had advanced 8 miles into North Korea to Yangyang, where command posts were established.

With remarkable determination, the ROKA 3rd Infantry Division advanced non-stop northward along the east coast. Averaging 15 miles a day, the expedition was, however, not without costly engagements with remnants of the KPA 5th Infantry Division. Enemy rearguard action persistently harried leading South Korean units, while groups of KPA troops bypassed by the South Koreans fell on ROKA supply points with anti-tank and mortar fire. The road had been heavily mined by the retreating North Koreans, resulting in large numbers of casualties to vehicle-borne South Korean troops. The ROKA Capital Division crossed the 38th close behind the 3rd Infantry Division, with elements splitting off to sweep the coastal Kŭmgang-san mountains.

Meanwhile, General MacArthur and his staff, while awaiting the green light to cross the 38th, continued to work on a two-pronged attack on the North Korean capital, P'yŏngyang. The UNC commander was adamant, for logistical and topographical reasons, that the US

An abandoned North Korean 76mm divisional gun M1942 (ZiS-3). (Photo NARA)

X Corps amphibious landing at Wŏnsan remain an integral element of his plan. The only passable east–west road connecting P'yŏngyang with Wŏnsan ran just north of the 38th Parallel. Farther north, the lofty, rugged Taebaek mountain range in central Korea would form a virtually impregnable barrier between the US Eighth Army to the west and the US X Corps to the east.

While the fight for the liberation of Seoul had raged, some of MacArthur's senior staff members gained the impression that MacArthur would place US X Corps under General Walker as soon as Seoul fell to UNC forces. Acting Chief of Staff Major General Doyle O. Hickey (while General Almond commanded US X Corps), Brigadier General Edwin K. 'Pinky' Wright of G-3 (operations) staff and Major General George L. Eberle, Far East Command G-4 (logistics), all had misgivings about the proposed split offensive plan, but failed to voice their concerns with their supreme commander. The final factor in MacArthur's decision-making process had been North Korea's transport and communications infrastructure, crippled by weeks of USAF interdiction bombing.

On 29 September, General MacArthur endorsed a first draft outline of the operation, which allowed for the US X Corps to land at Wŏnsan twelve days after General Walker had passed through their Inch'ŏn–Seoul position.

The rest of Eighth Army, which, I presumed, was following me through the village [Munsan-ni] as easily as my platoon had. Down the road a mile or so I took a fork in the road and proceeded east, the 1st Cavalry Division in my wake. For the only time in my life I was in the first jeep on an advance and was the first American leading the division and Eighth Army into enemy-held territory. What a thrill!

About half a mile down the road, I received a frantic signal to stop. I was leading the Eighth Army down the *wrong* road. What a blow to my ego. What fun we had turning the whole regiment inside out along that narrow country road. I don't know why they didn't just have someone else at the rear of the column turn around and become the point, but they didn't. I had to resume the lead and the regiment had to back-and-forward its way until every vehicle was turned around and following the one it had followed before my gaffe. I passed everyone until I was again in the lead. I do not always understand Colonel [Marcel] Crombez [5th Cavalry Regiment CO], but, after all, I was only a second lieutenant.

Eighth Army's password that night was 'Wrong Road.'
Lieutenant Charles Payne, 3rd Battalion, US 19th Infantry Regiment*

---

* Donald Knox, *The Korean War, Pusan to Chosin: An Oral History.* (Harcourt Brace & Co., Orlando, 1985).

In pursuance of UNC Operations Order 2, on 3 October Walker issued operations orders for the role that his Eighth Army would play in the North Korea offensive. Upon securing a line west of the Imjin River with at least a division, US I Corps would assemble in the area where it would be relieved by US IX Corps. Here, the latter would be tasked with protecting the Seoul–Suwon–Taejon–Taegu–Pusan line of communication, while mopping up pockets of remaining North Korean forces in South Korea. Acting on army orders, US I Corps would then strike northward, with the US 1st Cavalry Division as vanguard. The US 24th and ROKA 1st divisions would protect the corps' flanks and be held in reserve.

ROKA II Corps, comprising 6th, 7th and 8th divisions, was ordered to central Korea to take up position between Ch'unch'ŏn and Ŭijŏngbu. A new South Korean division, the 11th, was to be activated by 5 October to assist US IX Corps to the rear.

On 5 October, the US 1st Cavalry Division headed north out of Seoul to secure the US I Corps assembly area just south of the 38th Parallel. That evening I Company spearheaded a US 5th Cavalry Regiment crossing of the Imjin River at Munsan-ni, north-west of Seoul.

Defeated North Korean troops emerge from their bunker. (Photo Corporal Robert Dangel)

At midday on 7 October, the US 16th Reconnaissance Company arrived at Kaesŏng, followed that evening by leading elements of the 1st Battalion, US 8th Cavalry Regiment (1/8th Cav). By last light the following day, the US 7th and 8th cavalry regiments had secured the Kaesŏng assembly area in strength, within shooting distance of the 38th. To the US 1st Cavalry Division's rear, the US 24th Infantry Division assembled in the Seoul area.

The small village of Lake Success on New York's Long Island, temporary home of the United Nations headquarters, had by early October become a global centre of attention as politician, diplomat and journalist alike waited for the General Assembly's decision on Korea's immediate future. On the morning of Sunday, 8 October, the world's newspapers declared an end to any speculation on the outcome:

MACA GETS A 'GO AHEAD' TO CROSS BORDER
United Nations General Assembly last night gave General MacArthur the 'go ahead' to cross the 38th Parallel (boundary line dividing North and South Korea) in pursuit of the fleeing Communist forces.

This was the effect of an eight-Power resolution passed by 47 votes to five, with eight abstentions. Only the Soviet Union and its supporters voted against. A Soviet motion for the withdrawal of all foreign troops from Korea was rejected by 45 votes to five.

Sir Benegal Rau, Indian delegate, told the Assembly of his country's 'gravest misgivings' over an occupation of North Korea by the United Nations. The result, he feared, might be to prolong North Korean resistance and even to extend the area of conflict.

The People, 8 October 1950

At this time, US military intelligence estimated that, at most, only 30,000 KPA troops had arrived back in North Korea since General Walker's breakout from the Pusan Perimeter. As the US Eighth Army commander's forces raced northward, around 3,000 soldiers of the KPA 6th and 7th divisions had been bypassed in the Kŭmch'ŏn and Taejŏn areas. The scant remnants of Major General Ch'oe Hyon's KPA 2nd Infantry Division had bombshelled into the hills north of Poun.

Elements of the KPA 9th and 10th divisions, pursued by units from the US IX and I corps, had withdrawn through Taejŏn, while to the east about 1,000 troops of the KPA 1st Infantry Division had retreated through Wŏnju and Inje.

From Choch'iwŏn, 24 miles north of Taejŏn, reports were received that the commander of the KPA I Corps, Lieutenant General Lee Kwon Mu, having replaced General Kim Ung, had closed his headquarters in the town before fleeing with members of his staff into the relative safety of the Taebaek mountains.

With the collapse of the Pusan front near Taegu, some 1,500 troops of the KPA 3rd Infantry Division had fled northward, crossing the 38th Parallel near Ch'unch'ŏn.

WE FIGHT ON, SAYS KIM SUNG

TOKYO, *Sunday.*

North Koreans are firmly resolved to continue the fight to ultimate victory under the support of the Chinese people, said North Korea's Premier, Kim Il Sung, today. In a broadcast congratulating Mao Tze-tung on the anniversary of the Chinese People's Republic, Premier Kim added: 'Our forces now fighting American Imperialists are deeply concerned about China and the Chinese.'

From Moscow it is reported the Chinese Communist Premier Chou En-lai said in a *Pravda* article today: 'China cannot remain indifferent to the fate of her neighbour's subjected imperialist aggression. The Korean people are fighting a long war and will be victorious in the end.

'The American Government is China's most dangerous enemy. American forces, now at China's frontiers, may expand their attack at any moment.'—A P.

Daily Herald, 2 October 1950

The division was able to reach P'yŏnggang—not to be confused with the North Korean capital P'yŏngyang—the northern apex of what became known by the UNC as the Iron Triangle. Ch'ŏrwŏn to the south-west and Kŭmhwa to the south-east completed the triangular North Korean and Communist Chinese concentration and communications hub, hotly contested throughout the conflict.

Of all the North Korean divisions that had invaded the south in June, none came closer to total annihilation than the KPA 13th. Only a handful of its troops finally made it back to the Iron Triangle. Throughout the remainder of September and well into October, stragglers from other disorganized KPA divisions continued to trickle back to North Korea: the 8th to the east of P'yŏnggang and on to the Yalu River, the 15th through Hongch'ŏn, the 12th and 9th along the central areas east of Seoul, and the 5th along the mountains of the east coast in the direction of Wŏnsan.

The majority of the North Korean army survivors concentrated in the Iron Triangle and the Hwach'ŏn–Inje area to the east, including KPA II Corps commander Lieutenant General Kim Kwang-hyop and the commanding general at the North Korean Army Front Headquarters at Kŭmch'ŏn.

As a matter of urgency, the North Korean military high command went about the reorganization and reconstitution of its forces, based largely around the remnants of those units that had managed to evade the UNC forces to return home. As September gave way

UN troops escort North Korean prisoners to holding camps in the rear. (Photo NARA)

to October, the Korean People's Army was being remoulded into a semblance of readiness for the inevitability of MacArthur crossing the 38th:

o   I Corps
Commanded by Lieutenant General Lee Kwon Mu.
17th and 46th divisions, and 105th Seoul Tank Division, operating in the Sukch'ŏn area.

o   II Corps
Commanded by Lieutenant General Kim Kwang-hyop.
2nd, 10th and 31st divisions, conducting guerrilla warfare in the Hwach'ŏn–Kŭmhwa–Yŏngdŏk area.

o   III Corps
Commanded by Lieutenant General Yu Kyong Su.
1st and 3rd divisions, based in central Korea from October 1950.

o IV Corps
Commanded by Lieutenant General Pak Chong Dok.
9th and, temporarily, 18th and 19th divisions, responsible for the defence of the Seoul–P'yŏngyang axis in September and October.

o V Corps
Commanded by Lieutenant General Pang Ho San.
6th, 7th, 12th, 38th and 43rd divisions, activated around September/October and deployed in the South P'yŏngang Province.

o VI Corps
Commander by Lieutenant General Ch'oe Yong Jin.
18th, 19th and 36th divisions, activated early in October and deployed to north-west North Korea.

o VII Corps
Commanded by Lieutenant General Lee Yong Ho.
13th, 32nd and 37th divisions, activated around September/October and sent for training in Manchuria.

o VIII Corps
Commanded by Lieutenant General Kim Chang Dok.
42nd, 45th and 46th divisions, activated in October and sent for training in Manchuria.

The British, arriving in South Korea from the Hong Kong garrison on HMS *Unicorn* and HMS *Ceylon* on 30 August, comprised the 1st Battalion Argyll and Sutherland Highlanders (1/Argylls), commanded by Lieutenant-Colonel G. L. Neilson, and the 1st Battalion, the Middlesex Regiment (1/Middlesex), commanded by Lieutenant-Colonel A. M. Man. The brigade was immediately moved to the front at Taegu where, on 2 September, they were placed under command of the US 1st Cavalry Division.

Ground support for US I Corps came from the 73rd and 89th tank battalions, the 9th and 90th field artillery battalions (FABs), and HQ Battery, 10th Anti-aircraft Artillery (AAA) and the 68th and 78th AAA gun battalions.

In the air, the US Fifth Air Force provided US I Corps with rolling close air support as the troops advanced. On the left flank, airborne Mosquito controllers conducted continuous reconnaissance sorties, calling in fighters to deal with impending enemy threats, including Lockheed F-80C Shooting Stars of the 8th Fighter Wing, the first US jet fighters to fly on operational service in the Korean War. The unit was based at the recently recaptured Suwŏn Air Base (K-13).

Lockheed F-80C Shooting Star fighters of the US 8th Fighter Bomber Wing, each armed with two 227kg bombs, on a sortie over Korea. (Photo USAF)

In spite of earlier intelligence sources indicating the presence of six KPA divisions, totalling 60,000 men, when the UN forces crossed the 38th it was quickly realized that only the KPA 19th and 27th infantry divisions defended the south–north Kŭmch'ŏn–Namch'ŏnjom axis north of Kaesŏng, in what was referred to as the Kŭmch'ŏn Pocket. The two former recently activated KPA brigades had only been expanded to divisional strength and status in September, and were yet to be blooded in combat. To the right of these divisions the 74th Regiment, KPA 43rd Infantry Division, was dug in on the west bank of the Yesong River, defending the crossing. The balance of the division had been tasked with the defence of the coastal zone to the west of the Yesong. To the east of Kaesŏng elements of the KPA 17th Armoured Division were in place just north of the 38th at Korangp'o-ri in the ROKA 1st Infantry Division sector.

By 29 September, the 3rd Battalion, Royal Australian Regiment (3RAR) had joined 27th Brigade, assembling at Taegu on 29 September to await brigade clearance orders. That same day, the brigade issued Order No. 1 'Ferret', informing battalion commanders of the presence of elements of the KPA 7th and 10th divisions across a 26-mile front north and south of Koryŏng. Brigade assessed the enemy's intention was to move on Taejon, or split into guerrilla groups.

With the US 2nd and 24th divisions on the brigade's respective left and right flanks, the three 27th Brigade battalions were tasked with the same 'clearance' responsibilities as the Americans:

a. Bn [battalion] areas will be covered and cleared by stages: from three to four miles daily.

b. Areas cleared will be actively patrolled the following day to ensure total absence of enemy. Where possible, civil police will be positioned in these areas, after clearance.

South Korean
General Paik
Sun-yup.

c.   Rd [road] patrols, where rd patrols are necessary, these will be carried out by
     day AND night. Bns will send out only one coy gp [company group] at present.*

Such company groups were to have a strength of a full or half a company. In support
would be three tanks from A Company, US 78th Tank Battalion, or three assault guns
from the US 6th Tank Battalion, a section of medium machine guns and a section of
3-inch mortars.

On 9 October, General Walker ordered his Eighth Army 'to strike out for P'yŏngyang
without delay'. From the vicinity of Kaesŏng, at 9 a.m., the US 1st Cavalry Division, commanded by Major General Hobart R. Gay, spearheaded the US I Corps across the 38th,
striking north in the centre for Kŭmch'ŏn. They were followed later that day by the 19th,
21st and 34th regiments of the US 24th Infantry Division. Commanded by Major General
John H. Church, the Americans struck westward for the port city of Chinnamp'o.

On the corps' right flank, the ROKA 1st Infantry Division under General Paik Sun-
yup moved on P'yŏngyang, while on the east coast, the ROKA I Corps jumped off with
Wŏnsan as its objective.

The British 27th Commonwealth Brigade (British 27th), under Brigadier Basil A. Coad
and with the newly attached 3RAR, led by Lieutenant-Colonel Charles Green, then crossed
the 38th Parallel, passing through the US 1st Cavalry Division in the centre to spearhead
the advance on Sariwŏn.

---

*   27th British Commonwealth Brigade War Diary, September to October 1950 (The Australia War
    Memorial Archives, Campbell).

2. DRIVE ON KŬMCH'ŎN

'A little thing like a night without fear is looked upon as a golden apple and about as rare.'

Captain Norman Allen, I Company, US 5th Cavalry,

about to cross the 38th Parallel[*]

The US 1st Cavalry Division's three regimental combat teams, having conducted short night and day reconnaissance patrols over the previous two days, began crossing the 38th Parallel on the morning of 9 October.

On the American division's right, the 5th Cavalry, commanded by Colonel Marcel G. Crombez, jumped off in a north-easterly direction to cross the parallel before doglegging to the west to join up with its two sister regiments to complete the envelopment of the North Koreans in the so-called Kŭmch'ŏn Pocket. However, the regiment's progress was slow, only arriving at the 38th at 7.30 p.m. that evening. Digging in for the night, at first light the next morning the crossing was made with hills commanding both sides of the road just north of the 38th Parallel unsecured.

After a night of consolidation and preparation, on the morning of 11 October the 1st Battalion, 5th Cavalry (1/5th Cav) jumped off. About 15 miles north-east of Kaesŏng, the battalion came under heavy enemy fire from three high points on an extended ridge overlooking a pass. The troops were forced to sit the night out until the next morning when the 2nd Battalion, 5th Cavalry (2/5th) arrived to join the fight. In the afternoon, the 5th Cavalry finally cleared the ridge of enemy soldiers. In an engagement with the North Koreans, a C Company platoon leader, First Lieutenant Samuel S. Coursen, while displaying remarkable bravery, lost his life in close-up combat with a group of enemy troops. For his actions, Coursen was posthumously awarded America's highest military decoration for valour, the Medal of Honor, as described in his citation:

1st Lt. Coursen distinguished himself by conspicuous gallantry and intrepidity above and beyond the call of duty in action. While Company C was attacking Hill 174 under heavy enemy small-arms fire, his platoon received enemy fire from close range. The platoon returned the fire and continued to advance. During this phase 1, his men moved into a well-camouflaged emplacement, which was thought to be unoccupied, and one was wounded by the enemy who were hidden within the emplacement. Seeing the soldier in difficulty he rushed to the man's aid and,

---

[*] Donald Knox, *The Korean War, Pusan to Chosin: An Oral History* (Harcourt Brace & Co., Orlando, 1985).

A US 1st Cavalry Division machine-gun team in action against a North Korean position, 1950. (Photo Army Center for Military History)

without regard for his personal safety, engaged the enemy in hand-to-hand combat in an effort to protect his wounded comrade until he himself was killed. When his body was recovered after the battle 7 enemy dead were found in the emplacement. As the result of 1st Lt. Coursen's violent struggle several of the enemies' heads had been crushed with his rifle. His aggressive and intrepid actions saved the life of the wounded man, eliminated the main position of the enemy roadblock, and greatly inspired the men in his command. 1st Lt. Coursen's extraordinary heroism and intrepidity reflect the highest credit on himself and are in keeping with the honored traditions of the military service.[*]

On the division's left, the 7th Cavalry, commanded by Lieutenant Colonel William A. Harris, struck westward to Paekch'on so as to jump off directly northward for the town of Hanp'o-ri to seal off the North Korean's rear. However, to achieve its objective, the regiment would have to traverse the heavily defended Yesong River crossing.

---

[*] Army Center of Military History, Washington.

Somewhere east of Kŭmch'ŏn, forward elements of the regiment had run into a roadblock and the column stopped. A little off the road lay several North Koreans who had been wounded in the fighting. Jerry Emer and another guy ate canned hamburger, a meal I detested so much that no matter how hungry I was, I refused to eat it.

A platoon of tanks hove into view. When they got closer, I saw the lead tank was led by a lieutenant wearing a Western-style moustache, goggles, and a baseball cap worn backward. He stood up in one of the hatches. When he spotted the North Koreans, he leaned forward to shout into the tank. This tank, followed by the other three, swerved off the road and clanked over the enemy soldiers. Shrill screams were quickly blotted out by the roar of the engines. A cloud of dust, mixed with blood, guts, and pieces of body swirled in the air.

The tanks returned to the road and were soon out of sight. Emer was a hardy soul and never missed a bite of his hamburger. The other kid vomited all over himself.
                    Private First Class James Cardinal, I Company, 5th Cavalry*

---

* Donald Knox, *The Korean War, Pusan to Chosin: An Oral History* (Harcourt Brace & Co., Orlando, 1985).

On 8 October, with the knowledge that the 7th Cavalry faced a major hurdle in crossing the Yesong River, General Gay had ordered intelligence and reconnaissance (I&R) patrols to be conducted to assess enemy strengths and the condition of the 800-yard-long high-level road/rail bridge over the river on the Kaesŏng–Paekch'on road. Upon inspection, the I&R platoon, despite coming under enemy mortar, automatic and small-arms fire from the west bank, concluded that, although still standing, the bridge would not be able to carry anything other than foot traffic. The platoon also reported that North Korean forces held the western side of the river from a point about a mile upstream from the bridge to the bay south of Yŏnan. Acting on this, regimental commander Colonel Harris ordered the 1st Battalion, 7th Cavalry (1/7th Cav) CO, Greek-born Lieutenant Colonel Peter Clainos, to seize the bridge and hold the crossing surrounds.

At midday, the 7th Cavalry laid down a three-hour artillery barrage onto enemy positions on the west bank of the Yesong. At 3 p.m. Clainos sent a platoon from C Company across the bridge, which it achieved with only a few casualties from enemy small-arms fire. As they dug in on the western approaches to the bridge, B Company, 8th Engineer Combat Battalion arrived on the bridge, working through the night under enemy fire to effect repairs to the road surface.

The rest of C Company followed, securing a hill to the right side of the bridge. B Company crossed next, taking the hill across the road from C Company. With the battalion largely now on the west bank, the artillery bombardment had to cease, at which point North Korean fire on the 1/7th Cav positions increased significantly. In a short space of time, the battalion had sustained seventy-eight casualties; C Company had seven killed and thirty-six wounded.

During the night, the North Koreans fell on the 1/7th Cav positions, prompting Harris at midnight to hasten the 2nd Battalion's (2/7th Cav) crossing of the bridge, which remained under enemy mortar and small-arms fire.

Once across, 2/7th Cav CO, Lieutenant Colonel Gilmon A. Huff, consolidated his battalion about 100 yards west of the bridge before moving in a column of companies down the road toward Paekch'on. After only a short distance, the enemy hit leading G Company's

M18 57mm recoilless rifle. (Photo Alf van Beem)

left flank. Heavy fighting ensued as Huff struggled to defend his position with 57mm recoilless rifles and 60mm mortars the heaviest support weapons at his disposal. Despite suffering a shoulder wound, Huff rallied his men through the night until first light revealed that the North Koreans had broken off their attack, leaving the way clear for the battalion to continue in their drive toward Paekch'on. That afternoon, the town fell to the 2/7th Cav, who passed through, seizing commanding high ground to the north.

The following morning—11 October—the 3rd Battalion, 7th Cavalry (3/7th Cav), commanded by Lieutenant Colonel Charles H. Hallden, crossed the Yesong. Twenty-four hours later, the battalion reached and secured its objective: the road and rail bridges over the Yesong at Hanp'o-ri. That evening, the 2/7th Cav also arrived at this position.

Closing the western escape route out of the Kŭmch'ŏn Pocket, a platoon from L Company, 3/7th Cav, set up a roadblock where they experienced the first indication of the division's pressure now being exerted on the trapped North Koreans. During the night eleven North Korean trucks, with lights on, drove into the Americans' ambush. Four trucks loaded with ammunition were destroyed and six seized. The North Koreans suffered around 100 casualties, including around 50 dead. Information gleaned from documents confiscated from a fatally wounded KPA regimental commander suggested that the North Koreans intended to stage a mass breakout from the cordon during the night of 14 October.

Jumping off from Kaesŏng, Colonel Raymond Palmer's 8th Cavalry launched its attack in between the 7th and 5th and along the central Kaesŏng–Kŭmch'ŏn axis, with the objective of skirting the KPA 19th and 27th divisions' right flank. But constant halting while engineers cleared landmines resulted in a snail's pace advance.

On 12 October, the regiment stopped once more when a heavily defended—tanks, self-propelled guns and anti-aircraft weapons—North Korean stronghold was encountered. Colonel Palmer called for air and artillery support, but the ensuing airstrike by sixteen aircraft and a bombardment from 155mm howitzers seemed to have little impact on the enemy position. The 1st Battalion, 8th Cavalry (1/8th Cav) commanding officer, Colonel Robert W. Kane, was seriously wounded during the fight, necessitating his evacuation.

The previous day, at first light the ROKA 1st Infantry Division, commanded by the 30-year-old General Paik Sun-yup, crossed the Imjin River at Korangp'o-ri. Crossing the parallel to the US 1st Cavalry Division's right, the South Koreans struck north-west, converging with the 5th Cavalry late on 12 October while the latter was in combat with a unit of North Koreans. From this point, the 5th Cavalry took precedence on the northward road before branching off to the left in the direction of Kŭmch'ŏn. Following behind, with tanks of C Company, 6th Medium Tank Battalion in support, General Paik continued his advance on Sibyŏn-ni to the north. From there, he was to jump off to the north-west for P'yŏngyang.

*

Although very little is known about the enemy's order of battle, it is believed that elements of 27 North Korean Brigade are in our area. All ranks are most eager to meet their counterpart Brigade of the North Korean Army and impart on them some good British Army and Australian Army infantry lessons.

If contact is made, it is hoped that the Brigade will no longer have any rivals in the North Korean Army bearing the same number.

Brigadier B. A. Goad DSO,
CO 27th British Commonwealth Brigade, 13 October 1950[*]

---

[*] 27th British Commonwealth Brigade War Diary, September to October 1950 (The Australia War Memorial Archives, Campbell).

By the beginning of October, the 27th British Commonwealth Brigade—including 3RAR—had been operating in a 500-square-mile area of responsibility to the north and west of Kŭmch'ŏn on the outer fringes of the former Pusan Perimeter.

On 3 October, Brigadier Coad received a warning order from US I Corps to get ready to move, but without divulging any detail. The following day, the brigade was ordered to concentrate by 8 a.m. in readiness to move to an assembly area 'north of Seoul'. Brigade headquarters, rear echelon personnel, equipment and stores would go by road, while the three battalions would be airlifted from Taegu to the Kimp'o airfield in Fairchild C-119 'Flying Boxcar' and Douglas C-47 'Skytrain' military transports. The brigade and three battalion commanders moved overland to Kimp'o.

During the morning of 9 October, having faced unforeseen logistical problems, the 27th British married up at a designated staging area 12 miles from Seoul. Now under command of the US 1st Cavalry Division, on the morning of 10 October, Brigadier Goad visited divisional HQ for a final briefing before crossing the parallel. The brigade was to prepare to take over from the 5th Cavalry, advancing north-east from Kaesŏng and across the parallel, following the same route taken earlier by the 5th Cavalry.

As leading battalion, during the day the 1st Battalion, Middlesex Regiment (1/Middlesex), concentrated 2 miles east of Kaesŏng, where, as follow-up battalion, they were later joined by 3RAR. At the same time, the 1st Battalion, Argyll and Sutherland Highlanders (1/Argylls), concentrated near brigade HQ in Kaesŏng.

In support of the brigade, the 6th Tank Battalion arrived, equipped with M-46 Patton tanks. Artillery support followed in the form of the US 90th Field Artillery Battalion with 155mm howitzers.

The next day, orders were changed so that the 27th British would now follow the 5th Cavalry before advancing westward on Kŭmch'ŏn. The latter would continue to the north to encircle the North Koreans in the pocket.

A US 6th Tank Battalion discharges its turret gun. (Photo NARA)

1/Middlesex was now ordered to follow and close in on the 5th Cavalry, but the brigade was beset with problems from the start. Issued with highly inaccurate 1:50,000 maps of Korea, 1/Middlesex came to a sudden halt when the axis of advance track ended abruptly. At Kaesŏng, 3RAR were forced to remain in the concentration area due to insufficient troop transport.

Early on 12 October, 1/Middlesex stalled once more when it ran into the 5th Cavalry's tail. At the same time, 3RAR closed in on 1/Middlesex's rear, while elements of the ROKA 1st Infantry Division swung in front of the 5th Cavalry. In the ensuing congestion and confusion, the 27th British was ordered to stop its advance, pending withdrawal and deployment to another sector.

For the 27th British, the following day—13 October—was equally void of any significant advances. Brigadier Coad had received new orders in the morning to clear the area 7 miles north-west from the starting point of enemy troops. Early in the afternoon, 1/Middlesex and 3RAR were withdrawn to concentrate in the initial jump-off point, to be rerouted. As the day drew to an end, C and D companies from 3RAR, with a platoon of four Sherman tanks and HQ Battery, US 13th FAB, in support, had only advanced 3,000 yards.

To the north, the 7th Cavalry blocked the northern exit road from Kŭmch'ŏn, while the 5th and 8th Cavalry attempted to tighten the cordon from the east and south. From the direction of Sibyŏn-ni, the 5th Cavalry came up against an expansive minefield with around 300 North Korean troops in ambush. However, the resistance was quickly neutralized, and as the sun set, the Americans were only 8 miles from their objective.

In the centre, the 8th Cavalry encountered the main concentration of enemy troops in the pocket. Despite artillery preparation and air-to-ground fighter support at thirty-minute intervals, large numbers of troops of the KPA 19th and 27th infantry divisions retaliated with aggressive tank, mortar, artillery and small-arms counterattacks. In one such attack, enemy T-34 tanks fell on an outpost manned by B Company, US 70th Heavy Tank Battalion.

One T-34 escaped, and while the other two North Korean tanks burned, the Americans dug in for the night. The following morning, the company renewed its advance. Sergeant Harris continues his account:

As our tank approached the M-26 tank that had hit the land mine on 12 October, we started to receive antitank fire from across the river. We fired one round of high explosive (HE) and quickly eliminated the antitank gun.

By 0400 hours on 13 October, a heavy fog had moved in and I could hardly see the end of the gun tube. I was on turret duty and Captain Frazer was resting in the gunner's seat. I awakened him because I heard the track sounds of a Russian T-34 tank coming down the road. I quickly returned to the driver's position and as I dropped down in my seat, there was the sound of a large crash.

Actually, the enemy T-34 tank had run into the rear of Sgt, Drewery's M-4 [M4A3E8 Sherman variant] tank and was trying to push it off the road. It backed up and then attempted to push it again. By radio, Captain Frazer told Sgt. [Marshall] Drewery to let him push his tank again and a short distance. The sergeant followed the captain's orders and let the enemy T-34 tank briefly push him. As the enemy T-34 backed off Sgt. Drewery's gunner fired one round which entered the barrel of the enemy 85mm and split the barrel wide open.

Then Captain Frazer ordered our gunner, Sgt. James Ward, to put a round of AP [armour piercing] into the enemy turret. Just as our tank fired, the other M-26 [Pershing] tank on the other side of the road fired on a second enemy T-34, which was about 200 yards up the road. The one shot hit its target and the enemy T-34 started to burn.

Sergeant James Harris[*]

---

[*] Edward L. Daily, *Strike Swiftly Korea: 70th Heavy Tank Battalion, 1950–1953* (Turner Publishing Company, Nashville, 1988).

A burnt-out North Korean T-34/85 tank. (Photo NARA)

After we passed by the disabled M-26 tank, we pulled into a large field. Suddenly, Company B was fired on by several enemy T-34 tanks, which were hidden behind the berm of an old railroad track. They would move slightly forward and fire at our M-26 tanks, and then move back, and then move up to fire again.

Company B quickly maneuvered into position as the tank battle exchanged rounds, firing at each other, at approximately eight hundred yards. The North Korean tankers were no match for our American tank personnel and M-26 tanks. It was almost like a shooting gallery as the five enemy T-34 tanks were completely eliminated. Furthermore, it was a terrific day for the 70th Heavy Tank Battalion, because seven enemy T-34 tanks and one antitank gun were destroyed; and we had no casualties. Also, this was a special day, because Korea is a land of many mountains and hill masses, and tank battles were unusual.[*]

At Kŭmch'ŏn, a miscellany of trucks and carts left the town with about 1,000 North Korean troops, heading north toward Namch'ŏnjom. At Hanp'o-ri, they ran into the 7th Cavalry roadblock at the Yesong River bridge. A firefight broke out immediately, in which air support was called in to assist. The North Koreans bombshelled in the direction of nearby hills, leaving behind 500 dead and 200 captured.

---

[*] Ibid.

US 105mm howitzer. (Photo Jud McCranie)

Farther west, on the morning of 13 October, elements of the KPA 43rd Infantry Division, cut off to the east of Paekch'on, ambushed the rear of the 7th Cavalry advance, which included parts of the 1/7th Cav, HQ Battery, US 77th FAB and B Company, US 8th Engineer Combat Battalion. When news of the desperate situation reached the 3/21st blocking position HQ at Paekch'on, commanding officer Lieutenant Colonel John A. McConnell rushed I Company to the ambush site. Under heavy fire from the American infantry, the North Koreans disengaged and fled, but the damage had been done. Initial reports revealed that the Americans lost twenty-nine killed—the vast majority from the 77th FAB—and thirty wounded. The Korean War Project roll of Honour for the 77th FAB on 13 October 1950, in what is referred to as the 'Paekchon Ambush', lists thirty-three killed in action.*

The South Koreans suffered eight killed and four wounded. A total of eighteen vehicles were either destroyed or damaged. In a second ambush that night, the North Koreans captured twelve men from the 2/7th, of whom six later escaped.

Shortly after midnight on 14 October, the 2/5th Cav closed in on Kŭmch'ŏn. After clearing a North Korean position on the outskirts of the town, the battalion secured the

---

* Korean War Project, www.koreanwar.org/.

THE STORY OF KOREA'S LIFE-STRUGGLE

When husband and wife quarrel, or old friends part in Korea, people say: 'A 38th Parallel has been drawn between them.'

So said Dr Whang-Kyung Koh, woman Professor of Sociology at Seoul University and Director of Seoul's Women's Institute and Bureau, to members of Sunderland's United Nations' Association last night. She told of the ancient Korean civilization— it goes back 4,283 years in legend—its progress through the middle ages—they had iron-clad battleships in 1592—and the invasions which ravaged the land.

Left In Ruins
Japanese invaded in the 16th Century. After years of war they left the country in ruins. So, for 300 years Korea barred her frontiers to everyone but China, for the sake of peace. And that is partly why so little of Korea—12th largest nation in the world: sixth in Asia—was so little known to Western civilization. But the Japanese returned in 1910 and stayed 35 years. They banned universal education from this land of culture.

Premature
At the war's end Koreans celebrated independence, said Dr Koh. But prematurely—for Russian and American armies became the two new masters in place of the old one. Eventually freedom came for the South. Ever since the 38th Parallel was drawn as a border between north and south we Koreans having been sitting on dynamite. After this war nothing will be left of Korea but blood and dust, said Dr Koh.

Sunderland Daily Echo and Shipping Gazette, 14 October 1950

northern urban area. A while later, the 3/5th Cav took the southern part. At 8.30 a.m., Colonel Crombez arrived with his regimental command and staff.

With the 1/5th Cav kept back to hold the town, the 2/5th Cav was immediately ordered to strike northward to link up with the 7th Cavalry at Hanp'o-ri. As the battalion approached the small town, an estimated 2,400-strong North Korean force broke off its attack on elements of the 7th Cavalry, before dispersing into nearby hills to avoid capture.

At the same time, Crombez instructed the 3/5th Cav to continue south on the Kaesŏng road to effect a junction with the northward-advancing 8th Cavalry. Around noon, the battalion met up with an 8th Cavalry special task force at the head of the regiment 4 miles south of Kŭmch'ŏn. In a space of five days, General Gay's US 1st Cavalry Division had completed the envelopment of the pocket, but by then—14 October—large numbers of North Korean troops had managed to slip the net and escape to the north and north-west.

*

Across the Pacific in Washington, on the afternoon of 11 October 1950, President Harry S. Truman boarded *The Independence* on the first leg of his historic visit to the remote Wake Island where he would meet with General MacArthur to discuss the situation in Korea. The Douglas VC-118 Liftmaster was a bespoke military version of the DC-6 commercial airliner that Truman had named after his hometown in Missouri. Secretary for the Army Frank Pace, JCS Chairman General Omar N. Bradley and an entourage of top military and Whitehouse staff followed in a Lockheed C-121 Constellation.

It was not a national secret that America's chief executive and the supreme commander of United Nations forces in Korea were poles apart in the determination and implementation of war policies. The publicity-seeking general, when refused authorization for the use of nuclear bombs against the North Koreans, made a public statement essentially accusing Washington of 'appeasement'. MacArthur's policies and designs on the prosecution of the war often flew in the face of both the president and the Joint Chiefs of Staff, revealing his disdain for Washington's authority.

After stopping at Lambert Field, St Louis, the Fairfield-Suisun Air Force Base in California and the Hickam Air Force Base on Oahu, Hawaii, Truman arrived on the Pacific coral atoll known as Wake Island early in the morning of 15 October. There were some among the scores of waiting reporters and journalists, who had arrived earlier on a separate flight, who noticed that MacArthur did not salute the president, his commander-in-chief.

As the conference convened, MacArthur delivered a gilt-edged—some would argue arrogant—resumé of the war:

I believe that formal resistance will end throughout North and South Korea by Thanksgiving [23 November]. There is little resistance left in South Korea—only about 15,000 men—and those we do not destroy, the winter will. We now have 60,000 prisoners in compounds.

In North Korea, unfortunately, they are pursuing a forlorn hope. They have about 100,000 men who were trained as replacements. They are poorly trained, led and equipped, but they are obstinate and it goes against my grain to have to destroy them. They are only fighting to save face. Orientals prefer to die rather than to lose face.[*]

---

[*] *Substance of Statements made at Wake Island Conference*, 15 October 1950, compiled by General Omar N. Bradley, Harry S. Truman Library and Museum.

Above: US President Harry S. Truman on the steps of his aircraft *The Independence*. (Photo Abbie Rowe)

Right: President Truman awards the Distinguished Service Medal, Fourth Oak Leaf Cluster, to General McArthur, Wake Island conference. (Photo US Navy Signals Corps)

The sprawling K-10 airfield at Chinhae. ('Horse' Sweeney)

The culmination of the highly orchestrated and choreographed Wake Island public relations exercise took place in San Francisco on 17 October 1950 when, during an address, Truman extolled the 'superb achievements' of American forces in Korea, adding: 'It is also a source of pride to us that our country was asked to furnish the first commander of United Nations' troops. It is fortunate for the world that we had the right man for this purpose—a man who is a very great soldier—General Douglas MacArthur.'[*]

Six months later, President Truman would relieve the general he once referred to as 'Mr Prima Donna, Brass Hat, Five Star MacArthur' of his commands for being unable to 'give his wholehearted support to the policies of the United States Government and of the United Nations in matters pertaining to his official duties'.[†]

---

[*]   Log of President Truman's Trip to Wake Island, 11–18 October 1950, Harry S. Truman Library and Museum
[†]   Truman Library Institute blog, 11 April 2016.

3. EASTERN OFFENSIVE

'Unless and until the enemy capitulated, I regard all of Korea open for our mil operations.'
General Douglas MacArthur[*]

Through the months of August and September 1950, UNC forces along the P'ohang–Yŏnil–An'gong-ni axis, largely comprised of South Korean divisions, endured prolonged, bitter North Korean attacks on the integrity of the Pusan Perimeter in that sector.

During the hours of darkness on 16 August, LSTs evacuated more than 11,000 men of the 22nd and 23rd regiments, ROKA 3rd Infantry Division, commanded by Brigadier General Kim Baik Yil, and South Korean National Police, together with the division's arms and equipment. The battered units were landed south of P'ohang to consolidate for a counteroffensive to remove the KPA 5th and 12th divisions from positions to the north and north-west of the port city.

Typical of his mobile defensive tactics, early in September General Walton committed elements of the US 24th and 2nd divisions and the US 73rd Tank Battalion to prop up the flagging ROKA I Corps front. But his hoped-for instant remedy failed to materialize as the ROKA 3rd Infantry Division commander, Brigadier General Kim Suk Won, and his two deputies deserted their posts by claiming to be ill. Walker relieved Kim and the ROKA I Corps commander and placed Major General John H. Church in command of all operations in the east. By 15 September, the UNC forces had reclaimed the initiative and started pushing largely spent North Korean forces northward.

After initial setbacks, and with heavy fire support from the air and the battleship USS *Missouri* off P'ohang, by 22 September the ROKA 3rd Infantry Division had captured Hunghae on the east coast, rolling back the KPA 5th Infantry Division toward Yŏngdŏk in complete disarray.

Thus along its length, by 23 September, the Pusan Perimeter cordon had ceased to exist as the whole North Korean army limped back in the direction of the 38th Parallel. Church took his division back to Taegu.

Jumping off from Ŭisŏng in the ROKA II Corps sector, the ROKA 6th and 8th divisions, rejuvenated by fresh successes, started out on a rapid march toward the 38th Parallel, pushing back the KPA 8th and 12th divisions ahead of them. However, in their haste and by bypassing strong enemy resistance at Chech'ŏn and Wŏnju, the South Koreans left the rear vulnerable to attack.

---

[*] Top Secret memo to the JCS, 30 September 1950. Harry S. Truman Library and Museum.

The Iowa-class American battleship USS *Missouri* (BB-63) at anchor in the Sea of Japan, 1950. (Photo US Navy)

In their desperation to escape to the north, during the night of 1/2 October, an estimated 2,000 North Korean troops overran the ROKA II HQ at Wŏnju, inflicting heavy casualties on corps staff. Five attached American officers also lost their lives in the surprise attack. The North Koreans spent the rest of the hours of darkness slaughtering an estimated 1,000 to 2,000 civilians in an orgy of unbridled brutality.

On the eastern seaboard, the Capital and 3rd divisions of the ROKA I Corps, with support from US naval fire from offshore stations, caught the KPA 5th Infantry Division completely unawares, taking Yŏngdŏk on 25 September. The North Koreans bombshelled into the mountains where they split into independent guerrilla gangs. By the end of the month, the ROKA 3rd Infantry Division was in striking distance of the 38th Parallel.

The overriding priority for the depleted and scattered North Korean army had become that of implementing the most expedient and safest route back home. Along the coast, remnants of the KPA 5th Infantry Division re-mustered to fall back on Wŏnsan, closely followed by the ROKA Capital and 3rd divisions.

By 9 October, the two ROKA divisions had advanced 110 miles north of the 38th, and on the southern approaches to Wŏnsan. During the day, the ROKA Capital Division captured large quantities of war matériel and supplies, 6 tanks, 4 artillery pieces, 10 82mm mortars,

1 120mm mortar, 30 heavy machine guns, 500 submachine guns and 5,000 Russian-made rifles. To the right, the ROKA 3rd Infantry Division was slowed by enemy artillery fire from elements of the KPA 24th Mechanized Artillery Brigade. As the North Koreans withdrew, they maintained an artillery bombardment of the city centre. Later that day, the 23rd Regiment, ROKA 3rd Infantry Division, secured the airfield, at which their first air resupply arrived on 12 October.

On 11 October, the South Koreans secured Wŏnsan, their speed of execution so rapid that MacArthur, while planning an Inch'ŏn -style amphibious landing at the port city, was wrong-footed. However, the questionable planning of Operation Tailboard proceeded apace, with the US X Corps yielding control of the Inch'on–Seoul area to the US Eighth Army so as to prepare for the Wŏnsan landing.

The port of Wŏnsan was, for MacArthur, of significant strategic importance. The city was a key hub on the main sea and rail supply line from Vladivostok in the Soviet Union. As the eastern terminus of the lateral highway across the peninsula, Wŏnsan was one of two major North Korean military supply depots in the country. It therefore was a selected site for large-scale troop training and a staging area for the inland shipment of war matériel.

On 1 October, Joint Task Force 7 (JTF 7), commanded by Vice-Admiral Arthur D. Struble, had been reactivated to land Major General Edward M. Almond's US X Corps at Wŏnsan. The US 1st Marine Division and US X Corps headquarters were to embark at Inch'ŏn, while the bulk of the corps' troops and the US 7th Infantry Division would outload at Pusan.

The US 1st Marine Division Operation Order 16-50, issued on 15 October reflected elements of planning not dissimilar to Operation Chromite, the Inch'ŏn landing a month earlier. The task of landing and securing a beachhead to cover the landing of the rest of the US X Corps was given once more given to the US 1st Marine Division. Regimental Combat Teams (RCTs) 1 and 7 would spearhead the invasion by landing on designated Yellow and Blue beaches respectively. The 5th Battalion, ROKA Korean Marine Corps (KMC) was attached to RCT-1 and the ROKA 3rd Battalion to RCT-7. RCT-5 would be kept in reserve until ordered to land on Blue Beach. The US 11th Marine (Artillery) Regiment (reinforced) and C and D companies, 1st Tank Battalion, would follow.

The US 7th Infantry Division was to depart from Pusan on 20 October to land at Iwŏn farther north on the coast nine days thereafter.

Earlier in the month, military intelligence assessed enemy strengths and dispositions in the Wŏnsan objective zone. However, the disorganized generally northward movement of enemy troops throughout the peninsula to the north of the 38th Parallel made accuracy problematic.

It was known that the 4,000-strong KPA 42nd Infantry Division, comprising the 76th and 96th regiments, had been organized at Wŏnsan on 5 September.

SOUTH KOREANS 55 FROM WONSAN

Red Columns Moving South From Manchurian Border
While General MacArthur's American troops north of Seoul continued to regroup yesterday without any indication of a west coast drive over the 38th Parallel to the Communist capital Pyongyang, 100 miles away on the east coast two South Korean divisions, 40 and 30 miles respectively beyond the Parallel, drove on towards the big port of Wonsan, 55 miles to the north, which could become a useful supply base.

'We will go through to the Manchurian border,' the chief of staff of one of the South Korean divisions said: 'It will take a month or two months, but we will be there before the winter.' More than 30 United States officers and men are with the invading South Koreans as an advisory group.

Stalin's Picture Smashed
Jubilant North Korean civilians smashed pictures of Stalin and North Korean Premier Kim Ir Sen and burned them in the streets yesterday as the South Korean Third Division advanced along the east coast of North Korea with a speed that amazed its U.S advisers.

South Korean President Syngman Rhee, interviewed in Seoul, expressed belief that South Korean troops crossed the 38th Parallel without orders from the U.S. Eighth Army. 'I don't believe the Eighth Army will force them to come back,' he said

Northern Whig, 4 October 1950

The US 7th Infantry Division stockpiling fuel and supplies at the Iwŏn beachhead, October 1950. (Photo NARA)

The KPA 1st Marine Regiment, with a strength of around 1,200, had been tasked with coastal defence around the harbour. Between six and twelve 122mm field guns had been emplaced. In addition, there were known anti-aircraft positions around the harbour. Whilst the port was the principal North Korean naval base, the unit had failed to enter combat.

To the south, it had been reported that remnants of the KPA 18th Infantry Division and the KPA 25th Brigade had been ordered to consolidate in the Ch'ŏrwŏn area, a sector controlled by the ROKA I and II corps. A viable threat from the north was not considered probable.

However, a more organized KPA 23rd Infantry Division, supported by artillery and armour, together with fresh units from Manchuria, presented a plausible threat to the Wŏnsan landing.

By far the greatest obstruction to the success of Operation Tailboard was the estimated 4,000 Soviet-made magnetic and contact mines—some dating back to 1904—scattered throughout Wŏnsan's sea approaches. The mines were predominantly of two types: the Soviet MKB chemical horn contact mine and the Model 1926 (M-26) inertia contact mine.

South Korean minesweeper *512* detonates a Soviet-type contact mine off Wŏnsan, October 1950. (Photo NARA)

A veteran of the Pacific Theatre and commander of Mine Forces Pacific just before the Japanese surrender, Admiral Struble felt understandable apprehension. North Korean naval forces had been well supplied by the Soviet Union and China with all sorts of sea mines and they were used as much as possible to defend Wonsan. During the Korean War, naval mines laid by North Korean forces caused 70 per cent of the casualties sustained by the US Navy, and caused four vessels to sink.

On 26 September, while shelling the shore off Korea, the Allen M. Sumner-class destroyer USS *Brush* (DD-745) struck a mine while steaming off Tanch'ŏn, causing major damage to her midships section and breaking her keel. Thirteen men were killed and thirty-one injured. Limping under escort from the cruiser USS *Worcester* (CL-144), the destroyer USS *DeHaven* (DD-727) and the salvage tug USS *Bolster* (ARS-38), it took Commander Fletcher L. Sheffield, the ship's captain, four days to coax *Brush* the 470 miles to the nearest safe port at Sasebo Naval Base, Japan.

Two days later, the wooden-hulled South Korean minesweeper ROKS *Gapyeong* (YMS-509, formerly USS YMS-220) hit a mine and sank, killing twenty-six of her crew.

On 30 September, the destroyer USS *Mansfield* (DD-728) struck a mine while searching for a crashed USAF B-26. Casualties amounted to five missing and forty-eight injured. While navigating the channel into the North Korean harbour of Chosŏn, 60 miles north of the 38th Parallel, at around 2.50 p.m. the destroyer USS *Lyman K. Swenson* (DD-729) had stopped at the 50-fathom curve while *Mansfield* steamed into 12 fathoms of water. Lookouts and officers on the bridge scanned the waters for any sign of the downed American aircraft and a designated mine lookout concentrated on the *Mansfield*'s path. None of the crew saw anything.

Soon after 3.30 p.m., a 'high-order' explosion occurred under the port bow of the ship. Captain Edwin Harvey Headland immediately backed both engines on full as the engineering officer rushed forward to assess damage and crew casualties. The watertight bulkhead forward at frame 48 where the mine had been detonated was shored up and pumping commenced to empty forward tanks to restore bow trim. Effective and swift damage control enabled Headland to safely steam *Mansfield* across the Sea of Japan to the dry docks at Sasebo.

The US Navy wooden-hulled, auxiliary minesweeper, USS *Magpie* (AMS-25) became the next victim, striking a floating mine at around 5 p.m. on 1 October. A massive explosion ripped through the vessel forward of the stack. She started to sink almost immediately, taking twenty-one of her crew, including commanding officer, Lieutenant Warren R. Person, down with her. Their bodies were never recovered and remain listed as missing in action. Only twelve members of the *Magpie*'s complement of thirty-three, all of them injured, survived.

At this point, Admiral Struble and his staff made the decision, as a matter of urgency, to form Advance Force JTF 7 to address the now very real threat in the Operation Tailboard

Mine-clearing off the Korean coast. (Photo US Navy)

objective area. A miscellany of American, Japanese and South Korean minesweepers and adapted marine vessels was committed for the task.

By this time, 24 miles of the 'Russian' channel from the 100-fathom curve had been cleared, leaving 10 miles to the inner harbour still to sweep. Passing between Yŏ-do (Ryŏ-do) and Hwangt'o-do islands, the channel had been used by Soviet shipping from the north.

On 11 October, Underwater Demolition Team (UDT) personnel from the high-speed transport USS *Diachenko* (APD-123) joined the exercise by searching for mines ahead of the sweepers.

General MacArthur's Wŏnsan D-Day, set for 20 October, left little time to complete the task. However, the capture of Wŏnsan by Brigadier General Kim Baik Yil's ROKA I Corps on 11 October largely removed the urgency. In a novel bid to speed up the process, early on the morning of 12 October, thirty-nine carrier-borne aircraft from USS *Philippine Sea* (CV-47) and USS *Leyte* (CV-32) pounded the channel with 1,000-lb. bombs.

Late morning on 12 October, US Navy minesweepers USS *Pirate* (AM 275), USS *Pledge* (AM 277), USS *Incredible* (AM 249), USS *Redhead* (AMS 34) and USS *Kite* (AMS 22)

A Martin PBM-5 Mariner from Patrol Squadron VP-47. (Photo US Navy)

swept near Sin-do Island and in the direction of the Kalma Pan-do peninsula. Directly overhead, a spotter helicopter of Marine Observation Squadron 6 (VMO-6) led the sweep, communicating with the sweepers through the high-speed minesweeper USS *Endicott* (DMS-35). A US Navy PBM-5 (Patrol Bomber, Martin) Mariner from US Patrol Squadron VP-47— 'The Golden Swordsmen'—provided added aerial observation.

As *Pirate* entered the uncleared sector at eight knots, her sonar picked up three mine lines ahead. The detection was confirmed by the helicopter spotter. After sweeping the area of twelve to sixteen mines, the ships retired to Sin-do Island as planned.

Suddenly and unexpectedly, *Pirate*'s sonar picked up a large number of contacts—a 'cabbage patch'—with the mines positioned at intervals of 50 yards. Ship's commander, Lieutenant Cornelius E. McMullen, quickly changed his heading to 245° to avoid the nearest mine. Moments later, a shallow mine was spotted just off the starboard bow, and at 12.09 p.m. *Pirate* detonated a mine. The explosion along frame 62 on the starboard side sent an enormous column of water into the air.

North Korean shore batteries at Kei-To and Soku-Semu immediately opened fire on the crippled ship. The other sweepers responded, targeting three of the enemy batteries, but by now *Pirate* was listing 20° to port. When the list approached 15°, Lieutenant McMullen had no choice but to order his ship to be abandoned. Less than five minutes after hitting the mine, *Pirate* slipped under the water completely, taking six seamen with her. Sixty crewmembers found themselves adrift in debris-strewn and oil-covered water where their ship had been only moments earlier. The North Korean batteries now turned their

Minesweeping off Wŏnsan. (Photo US Navy)

aim onto *Pirate*'s hapless survivors. For four hours accurate enemy fire hampered a complete rescue, during which many of the American sailors sustained shrapnel wounds—one man was killed.

Sister minesweeper USS *Pledge* was at this time engaging the enemy shore batteries with her single 3-inch gun in a bitter dual, during which she took an artillery hit. Almost immediately thereafter, at 12.20 p.m., *Pledge* struck a mine as her commander, Lieutenant Richard O. Young, ordered left full rudder, starboard engine, ahead two-thirds. The mine detonated amidships, on the starboard side, near the forward engine room. After about forty-five minutes of frantic efforts to seal hatches and save the *Pledge*, Lieutenant Young ordered the evacuation of his ship. Five of his crew lost their lives. Eventually, with air support from the USS *Leyte*, the enemy onshore batteries were silenced, but not before the USS *Redhead* sustained severe damage from direct enemy artillery hits and USS *Incredible* reported the loss of all her engines. That afternoon the US Navy suffered ninety-two casualties, killed missing and wounded.

Commander of the amphibious task force, Rear Admiral Allen E. Smith, summed up the day's events for Chief of Naval Operations, Admiral Forest P. Sherman,

WONSAN A CITY OF RUINS

Reuter's war correspondent, John Colless, to-day sent this description of liberated Wonsan from a hospital in Southern Japan. He was injured last night when flying 600 miles from Wonsan to file the report. Catching the airlift out of Wonsan, he flew to Kimpo, near Seoul, and then to Ashiha, Kyushu, Japan. There the aircraft hit the sea wall and crashed on landing. Two were killed and four passengers, including Colless, were injured.

Townspeople in Wonsan, he reports, said the Communists four days ago beheaded 500 Korean prisoners including women and children. When the fall of the town seemed inevitable the Communists executed them, and buried the bodies in the sands of the river.

Wonsan is now a city of ruins. Acres of the residential area are just smoking ashes. Big factories are gaunt, hollow skeletons or piles of rubble. A large oil refinery was completely wrecked by air bombing and the oil reservoirs are now a tangled mass of steel sheeting. Booty seized included 16 Russian-type Stormovik warplanes at Wonsan Airport. The Communists tried to destroy the planes by burning the hangars.

Dundee Evening Telegraph, 12 October 1950

in a single terse sentence: "We have lost control of the seas to a nation without a Navy, using pre-World War I weapons, laid by vessels that were utilized at the time of the birth of Christ."[*]

Admiral Sherman would later add his own conclusions:

Let's admit it, they caught us with our pants down. Those damn mines cost us eight days' delay in getting the troops ashore and more than two hundred casualties. That's bad enough. But I can all-too easy think of circumstances when eight days' delay offshore could mean losing a war.[†]

In the first week of October, the US 7th Infantry Division started the logistically onerous task of packing up and moving 13,500 troops and 1,500 tons of equipment and supplies 350 miles overland from Inch'ŏn to Pusan. Relieved of its blocking position at

---

[*] Tamara Moser Melia, *Damn the Torpedoes: A Short History of U.S. Naval Mine Countermeasures, 1777–1991* (Naval Historical Center, Washington, 1991).

[†] Malcolm W. Cagle and Frank A. Manson, *The Sea War in Korea* (Naval Institute Press, 2000).

US Marines come ashore at Wŏnsan. (Photo NARA)

Inch'ŏn, the US 17th Regiment was the last to leave on 8 October. Divisional HQ closed at Anyang-ni to reopen at Pusan. On 16 October, the division's advance command post was established aboard the Mount McKinley-class amphibious force command ship, USS *Eldorado* (AGC-11).

The previous day, the US 1st Marine Division had set off from Inch'ŏn for the 830-mile trip to Wŏnsan, its advance command post on board Rear Admiral James H. Doyle's flagship, USS *Mount McKinley* (AGC-7). When the Marines reached the objective area five days later landing was prevented by the ongoing mine-clearing operations. Admiral Doyle ordered the ships to steam up and down the coast while waiting for the all-clear to land, resulting in the Marines dubbing the repeated tedious action Operation Yo-Yo. According to the history, it was said, 'Never did time die a harder death, and never did the grumblers have so much to grouse about'.*

When the Marines did finally land at Wŏnsan—unopposed—on 25 October, they discovered that American entertainer Bob Hope had staged a show for the troops the previous evening and had left before the Marines walked ashore. The ROKA divisions had secured the city fifteen days ago and Marine air-maintenance crews had already reached Wŏnsan. The final insult, it is said, was the presence of South Korean troops on the beach 'welcoming' the Marines by showing them the middle finger.

---

* *Stars and Stripes* at www.stripes.com.

Arming 2 SAAF Squadron F-51D Mustangs at K-10. (Photo Syd de la Harpe)

At 10 a.m., on 27 October, the US 1st Marine Division shut down its command post on *Mount McKinley* and opened in Wŏnsan. Three days later, all the division's combat elements were on dry land.

Meanwhile at Pusan, the US 7th Infantry Division had also become frustrated by ten days of onboard inactivity. Eventually orders were received to move north, but General Almond, in view of the delay, had decided instead to land the division on the beaches at the town of Iwŏn, 150 miles north of Wŏnsan. This disembarkation point would bring the division considerably closer to its axis of advance along the Pukch'ŏng–P'ungsan–Hyesanjin road to its designated objective, the Yalu River on the border with Chinese Manchuria.

In pursuance of the changed plan, at Pusan the US 17th RCT had to transfer from the transports onto seven LSTs. After leaving on 27 October, the unit landed at Iwŏn on 29 October, where they found the approaches free of mines. The ROKA Capital Division on its relentless march up the east coast had taken and passed through the town a few days earlier. By 9 November, the whole of the US 7th Infantry Division had arrived and disembarked at Iwŏn.

Above: SAAF maintenance crew await the return of their aircraft from a sortie. (Photo Robin Anderson)

Right: A Model 1917 heavy machine gun in action in Korea. (Photo courtesy U.S. Army Center for Military History)

A US Marine M26 Pershing follows a line of prisoners of war down a village street, late September 1950. (Photo SSgt John Babyak, Jr.)

A 16-inch salvo from the USS *Missouri* at Chong Jin, Korea, in effort to cut KPA communications, 21 October 1950. (Photo US Navy)

4. P'YŎNGYANG FALLS

'And of course, there was the war in Korea, a war around which there had grown up such a political situation that military victory, at least a decisive military victory, was no longer in the cards.'

US President Dwight D. Eisenhower[*]

For the first two weeks of October 1950, at Inch'ŏn the logistical operation to outload the US 1st Marine Division for the Wŏnsan amphibious landing impacted directly on General MacArthur's drive on the North Korean capital, P'yŏngyang.

Port handling facilities were fully engaged with this exercise, which also demanded maximum commitment of road transport from US Eighth Army assistant chief of staff G-4 (logistics), Colonel Albert K. Stebbins. The cumulative knock-on effect was of major concern to US I Corps commander, Major General Frank W. Milburn. The ammunition supply depots at Kaesŏng found it increasingly difficult to maintain minimum stocks of 3,000 tons. Fuel supplies for corps armour was, on occasion, only guaranteed on a daily basis.

Lieutenant General Walton H. Walker was not prepared to risk committing more troops north of the Han River at Kaesŏng, and made the decision to hold US IX Corps south of the river until there was a significant improvement in supply-line reliability. When that situation materialized, the 5th and 11th regiments of the ROKA III Corps would relieve US IX Corps to join UN forces already in North Korea.

All the while, alternative lines of supply were being brought into operation to augment the 200 trucks daily transporting rations and fuel to supply points 50 miles north of Seoul. During October, an aviation fuel pipeline from Inch'ŏn to Kimp'o Airfield was completed. However, for some time it had been recognized that the ultimate solution lay in the rehabilitation of the 200-mile Pusan railway line from the old Pusan Perimeter at Taegu. The biggest task facing the engineers was the reconstruction of bridges, especially the large spans over the Naktong and Imjin rivers.

In a remarkable seven days, the 165-feet gap in the bridge over the Naktong at Waegwan was repaired, allowing rail traffic to cross on 5 October. Five days later, the line had been opened to the expansive Han River. Here, it would take a further eleven days to construct a 'shoofly' or detour bridge. This entailed lifting the damaged bridge deck and truss with hydraulic jacks and moving it to one side, then placing it on a set of temporary piers and temporary approach spans so that rail traffic could once more cross the Han into Seoul.

---

[*]   Address to the nation, 23 August 1954 (The Eisenhower Presidential Library).

South Korean troops move a 57mm anti-tank gun into position. (Photo US Army)

In yet another record-breaking operation, seventy Fairchild C-119 Flying Boxcar flights transported a 50-ton, 740-feet-long floating pontoon bridge from Japan to provide a vehicular crossing over the Han. On 30 September, more than 3,000 vehicles crossed the Han as the vital road link was re-established. But as General Walker's army continued northward into the North Korean heartland, the gap to the nearest railhead would remain at 200 miles.

Above the 38th Parallel, the so-called Kŭmch'ŏn Pocket operation to envelope North Korean troops was over, but with limited success as many enemy troops had slipped through the cordon. The town of Sariwŏn, just under halfway to P'yŏngyang was General Walker's next objective, but the onset of torrential rains had turned the already poor roads into quagmires of cloying mud. Plans to move the US 5th Cavalry ahead of the fleeing North Koreans had to be abandoned.

On 15 October, airstrikes on the town of Namch'ŏnjom softened the enemy stronghold in advance of the US 2/7th Cav that was heading north from Hanp'o-ri. Seizing the town at midday, after losing ten men killed and thirty wounded, the Americans discovered that the aerial attack had destroyed the KPA 19th Infantry Division command post, killing the chief of staff.

The next day the 3/7th Cav jumped off from Namch'ŏnjom, and by noon had covered the 17 miles north-west to take Sŏhŭng. The 1/7th Cav followed, striking north on

BRITISH TROOPS MAY STAY AFTER KOREA VICTORY

British troops in Korea may be used for anti-guerrilla work in reserve or on the country's northern frontier after the United Nations victory, Gen. Sir John Harding, Commander of British Far East Land Forces, said in Tokyo yesterday.

Gen. Harding, asked at a Press conference, whether he meant the British troops might be stationed on the Manchurian border, replied he did, but added: 'I don't see the troops sitting on the Manchurian border making faces at the Chinese on the other side.'

Their future role was a matter for Lt.-Gen. Walton Walker, U.N. Ground Commander, and a question of Gen. MacArthur's overall policy, he said.

Indo-China gets more Red aid
Reports from South China reaching Hong Kong yesterday said military supplies were flowing in greater quantities from Communist China to Ho Chi Minh's rebel forces in Indo-China. Ho Chi Minh, the rebel leader, was also reported to have visited Southern Kwangsi province recently and signed a friendship pact for military supplies which are being shipped from Canton to the Luichow peninsula, opposite Hainan Island. They are being moved by lorries across the border in the section recently evacuated by the French.

Birmingham Daily Gazette, 16 October 1950

a secondary road to dig in and prepare for an attack on Hwangju the next day. Late that afternoon, the recently appointed commander of the US 7th Cavalry, Colonel William A. 'Wild Bill' Harris, arrived in Sŏhŭng to establish the regimental HQ.

The 3RAR, now also arrived at Sŏhŭng, having been moved by US Army transport, to await the 1/Argylls and 1/Middlesex. The latest plan was for the brigade to pass through the 7th Cavalry to spearhead the division and to seize Sariwŏn. Brigade commander, Brigadier Basil Coad, recorded that it had rained throughout the night, and 'having turned suddenly cold, it was one of the worst nights spent in Korea yet'.[*]

Meanwhile on the US 1st Cavalry Division's right flank, the ROKA 1st Infantry Division, like their brothers in arms on the east coast, had made phenomenal progress. On 13 October, division commander, General Paik Sun-yup, had reached the strategically important crossroads at Sibyŏn-ni. Two days later, as he advanced

---

[*] 27th British Commonwealth Brigade War Diary, September to October 1950 (The Australia War Memorial Archives, Campbell)

Brigadier Basil Coad (left) and Lieutenant-Colonel Charles Green. (Photo Claude Rudolph Holzheimer)

north-east of Namch'ŏnjom, Paik encountered a regiment-strength pocket of North Korean troops just before the town of Miu-dong. With six tanks and artillery in support, the enemy put up a fierce resistance, until airstrikes were called in to assist. Ploughing ahead the next day—16 October—Paik took Suan, now only 40 air miles from P'yŏngyang.

Also on 15 October, a seemingly exasperated General Milburn looked to his left to gain momentum for the corps' advance on the North Korean capital. Major General John H. Church was ordered to move his US 24th Infantry Division into an attack position to the west of General Gay's cavalry. The first objective would be Sariwŏn—same as for the British 27th—and then make for P'yŏngyang to the north.

Jumping off from Paekch'on, Colonel Richard W. Stephens's US 21st Regiment encountered scattered pockets of resistance before reaching Haeju on 17 October, where 300 North Korean defenders were neutralized and the town captured. At the same time, the US 19th Regiment, under Colonel Ned. D. Moore, followed the US 5th Cavalry, heading west off the main highway at Namch'ŏnjom. However, movement on the road before the town was at a virtual standstill on 16 October as they became mired in a massive traffic jam with the 27th British and the US 19th Regiment. Despite orders from General Church, Colonel Moore could not leapfrog the 5th Cavalry.

In the situation, set against personal ambition and pride by both division generals to lead the corps in the attack on P'yŏngyang, rivalry inevitably led to acrimony and frayed nerves. Late on the afternoon of 16 October, the 7th Cavalry had reached Sŏhŭng where regimental HQ was established and a roadblock set up a mile to the south of the town. Colonel Harris gave the troops manning the roadblock orders to shoot at anything that moved to their front. Despite being instructed to inform 1/5th Cav to the south of this danger, the officer responsible failed to convey the message. At around 3 a.m., leading elements of the 1/5th Cav, mistaken for the enemy, were met by a hail of fire from the roadblock as they approached in the dark. Fire was returned as they too believed they had walked into a North Korean ambush. By the time the error was realized, seven troops of the 5th Cavalry had been wounded in the blue-on-blue exchange of fire.

On 17 October, the 7th Cavalry set off on a secondary road in a large arc from north of Sŏhŭng, with the intention of cutting the main P'yŏngyang road at Hwangju. At the same time, the 27th British, after passing through the 7th Cavalry in the morning, was to advance on Sariwŏn and the P'yŏngyang road some 30 miles to the west. From there the road and railway left the mountains to cross the open coastal plain to P'yŏngyang 35 miles to the north. Any North Korean defences could therefore be expected in the commanding heights before Sariwŏn.

After the 45-mile journey that was 'very tedious owing

A soldier of the 3rd Royal Australian Regiment in Korea. (Photo Australia War Memorial)

MEDAL OF HONOR

Private First Class, Robert Harley Young,
E Company, 8th Cavalry Regiment, US 1st Cavalry Division

Citation:
Pfc. Young distinguished himself by conspicuous gallantry and intrepidity above and beyond the call of duty in action.

His company, spearheading a battalion drive deep in enemy territory, suddenly came under a devastating barrage of enemy mortar and automatic weapons crossfire which inflicted heavy casualties among his comrades and wounded him in the face and shoulder. Refusing to be evacuated, Pfc. Young remained in position and continued to fire at the enemy until wounded a second time.

As he awaited first aid near the company command post the enemy attempted an enveloping movement. Disregarding medical treatment he took an exposed position and firing with deadly accuracy killed 5 of the enemy. During this action he was again hit by hostile fire which knocked him to the ground and destroyed his helmet.

Later when supporting tanks moved forward, Pfc. Young, his wounds still unattended, directed tank fire which destroyed 3 enemy gun positions and enabled the company to advance. Wounded again by an enemy mortar burst, and while aiding several of his injured comrades, he demanded that all others be evacuated first.

Throughout the course of this action the leadership and combative instinct displayed by Pfc. Young exerted a profound influence on the conduct of the company. His aggressive example affected the whole course of the action and was responsible for its success. Pfc. Young's dauntless courage and intrepidity reflect the highest credit upon himself and uphold the esteemed traditions of the U.S. Army.[*]

---

[*] Medal of Honor Recipients: Korean War, United States Army Center of Military History.

to the large number of convoys using the road',[*] at 10 p.m. on 16 October, Brigadier Coad mustered all his units in its assembly area 2 miles west of Sŏhŭng. Each of the three regiments had support units under their command. For 3RAR, this comprised

---

[*] 27th British Commonwealth Brigade War Diary, September to October 1950 (The Australia War Memorial Archives, Campbell).

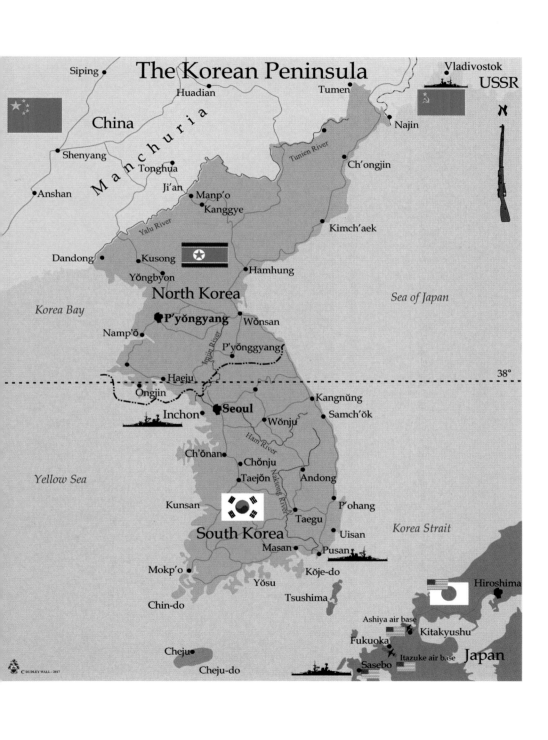

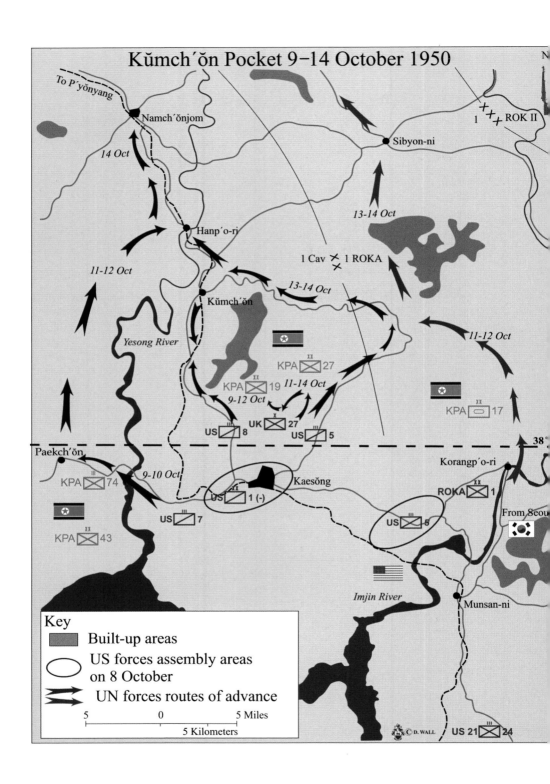

Kŭmch'ŏn Pocket 9–14 October 1950

To P'yŏnyang

Namch'ŏnjom

14 Oct

Sibyon-ni

13-14 Oct

Hanp'o-ri

11-12 Oct

1 Cav ✕ 1 ROKA

Kŭmch'ŏn

13-14 Oct

Yesong River

11-12 Oct

KPA ⊠ 27

KPA ⊠ 19   11-14 Oct

9-12 Oct

KPA ⊟ 17

US ⊠ 8   UK ⊠ 27

US ⊠ 5

Paekch'ŏn   38°

KPA ⊠ 74   9-10 Oct   Kaesŏng   Korangp'o-ri

US ⊠ 1 (-)   ROKA ⊠ 1

KPA ⊠ 43   US ⊠ 7   US ⊠ 8   From Seoul

Imjin River   Munsan-ni

Key

Built-up areas

US forces assembly areas
on 8 October

UN forces routes of advance

5   0   5 Miles

5 Kilometers

© D. WALL   US 21 ⊠ 24

1 ✛✛✛ ROK II

UN Forces Military Insignia

11th Airborne Division

187th ARCT
parachute wings

Tactical Air Command
USAF

187th ARCT

US Far East Air Forces

US Artillery
officers collar badge

US Fifteenth Air Force

US Armored Corps
collar badge

US Infantry Corps
collar badge

US Engineer Corps
collar badge

US Intelligence Corps
collar badge

US Transport Corps
collar badge

1st Bn Middlesex Regiment
cap badge
and shoulder title

1st Bn Argyll and Sutherland
Highlanders
cap badge and shoulder title

Australian Commonwealth
Military Forces
cap badge and shoulder title

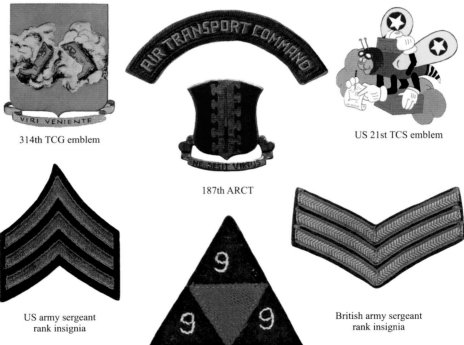

314th TCG emblem

US 21st TCS emblem

187th ARCT

US army sergeant
rank insignia

British army sergeant
rank insignia

27th British Commonwealth Brigade
formation patch - Korea 1950-51

Fairchild C-119 'Flying Boxcar' of the 314th Troop Carrier Group (at top) and UN military forces insignia.

M101A1 105mm howitzer (*above*) and M1 155mm howitzer (*below*). (Bottom photo Yaco Erisso)

North Korean propaganda poster depicting General MacArthur being forced off the Korean peninsula. (USMC)

Bell OH-13S Sioux, MASH workhorse of the Korean conflict (*above*) and a Sikorsky UH-19D Chickasaw in South Korean livery (*below*). (Top photo US Army, bottom photo Aeroprints)

'The Universal Soldier' Korean War Memorial, Battery Park, New York. (Photo Ron Cogswell)

D Company, US 89th Tank Battalion (Shermans), 2nd Platoon, US 72nd Engineer Combat Battalion, C Battery, US 90th FAB (155mm howitzers) and an American Air Contact Team (ACT) attached to the leading battalion.

At 6.30 a.m. on 17 October, Major David Wilson, officer commanding A Company, 1/Argylls, with a company platoon mounted on Sherman tanks, led the battalion out of Sŏhŭng. Assistant division commander, Brigadier General Frank A. Allen, accompanied the Scottish unit.

Just over an hour later, one of the Shermans destroyed an anti-tank gun as they passed the first line of hills. After 9 a.m., the Argylls encountered the first enemy resistance in the form of sporadic sniper fire as they entered the hamlet of Hŭngsu-ri. However, Wilson did not allow this to impede his rate of advance, knowing that 3RAR to his rear would address the matter.

At 12.30 p.m., 1/Argylls cleared a pass to reach Point 'Glenalmond' with 'speed and without incident'. Three miles from Sariwŏn, however, they were engaged by an estimated company-strength North Korean force positioned in an apple orchard overlooking the road at a distance of 200 yards. With tanks in support and galvanized by General Allen, the Argylls' A Company launched a successful counterattack.

Overhead, a spotter aircraft dipped its wings over the enemy to assist the tanks with fire direction. The ensuing fire flushed out a large group of North Koreans who sprinted for a ridge line to escape the killing zone. As they disappeared from sight, the Argylls cleared the area, finding around fifteen dead and seventy

The American M4A3(76) 'Easy Eight' Sherman tank used extensively in Korea. (Photo Beyond My Ken)

surrendered enemy soldiers. Ten machine guns, abandoned by the fleeing North Koreans, were also captured.

At 3.20 p.m., the battalion entered the bomb-damaged Sariwŏn, and an hour later Major Wilson signalled that the town had been secured. The battalion had sustained only four casualties, including one killed.

After 1/Argylls had jumped off from Sŏhŭng that morning, they were followed by a supporting battery of artillery, 3RAR with two artillery batteries and two companies of the US 89th Tank Battalion, brigade headquarters and to the rear, 1/Middlesex.

By late morning, 3RAR, advancing in US Army transport, was forced to harbour as it had caught up with the rear of the 1/Argylls column. At 6 p.m., the 3RAR motorized column passed through Sariwŏn and established battalion headquarters 4 miles north-west of the town. In an unlikely chain of events, however, it was destined not to be a peaceful night in Sariwŏn. Shortly after last light, 1/Argylls reported 'considerable' North Korean movement in and around the town.

Unwittingly, and without the benefit of knowledge, elements of a KPA division were being corralled from three directions by UN forces: the 18th Regiment, US 24th Infantry Division from the south, the US 7th Cavalry the north and the 27th British the east. The only possible route of escape for the North Koreans was through Sariwŏn.

Street battles broke out in the town, in often surreal situations of mistaken identity. In the dwindling light, the North Koreans mistook 3RAR and 1/Argylls for Soviet soldiers, even to the extent of exchanging greetings. The UN forces took the KPA troops in front of them to be South Koreans leading the main US 24th Infantry Division. Bizarrely, there were occasions when truckloads of antagonists found themselves parked next to each other.

Commanding officer of the 1/Argylls, Lieutenant-Colonel Leslie Neilson and Major J. Sloan of the 1/Argylls, travelling in the semi-darkness through Sariwŏn's southern reaches, drove into the middle of a twin column of advancing North Korean troops, the latter unaware that the town had fallen to UN forces. With reversing not an option, Neilson shouted at his driver to accelerate. After 5 miles, the extremely lucky CO and his driver left the enemy column behind and found concealed shelter off the road for the night.

Around midnight, a semblance of order returned to Sariwŏn. An estimated 200 North Koreans had lost their lives in scattered exchanges of fire, but the bulk of the column passed through the town. There the 3RAR roadblock, with Major Ian Bruce Ferguson (soon to be CO of the battalion) in attendance, persuaded 2,000 North Koreans to lay down their arms.

Earlier that day, while the 27th British was still advancing on Sariwŏn, the 1/7th Cav, under Lieutenant Colonel Peter Clainos, spearheaded the regiment's advance along poor roads toward Hwangju.

GALLANTRY IN KOREA

Brigadier awarded C.B.E.
The following awards for services in Korea were published in the "London Gazette" last night:

C.B E.—T/Brigadier Basil Aubrey Coad. D.S.O., late infantry.

Bar to the Military Cross—Captain John Albert Penman. M.C., T.D., the Argyll and Sutherland Highlanders (Princess Louise's).

Brigadier Coad, the citation says, took his brigade to Korea at very short notice. 'It was engaged with the enemy within a few days of arrival and has distinguished itself in every operation in which it has taken part. His conduct has undoubtedly been a fine example and an inspiration to all ranks under his command.'

Brigadier Coad, 43-year-old son of a Royal Navy engineer captain, won the D.S.O. in France in 1944 and a bar at Arnhem.

Captain Penman heard that a jeep had overturned and that a British officer was lying seriously injured nearby. Accompanied by three other ranks he went forward to the jeep and brought back the injured officer safely. While engaged in this he was under small-arms fire directed at him for approximately 15 minutes.

Captain Penman has been twice wounded in Korea, once in mid-September and again early in November. Since then he has been promoted to major. He won the M.C. in 1940 when, as a second lieutenant, he helped to beat off an ambush of his unit's convoy on the retreat to Dunkirk.

Belfast News-Letter, 6 December 1950

As the Americans neared their objective, orders were received for the 1/7th Cav to turn south at Hwangju to assist the 27th British with trapping large numbers of North Koreans spotted near Sariwŏn. The 2/7th Cav would hold Hwangju.

Heading south on the Sariwŏn–P'yŏngyang highway, leading elements of 1/7th Cav captured a North Korean cavalry unit together with thirty-seven horses. Farther down the road, the battalion came under enemy fire from a hill to their front. Confusion again arose as to who the North Koreans thought they were facing. Believing the Americans to be a Soviet column, the North Koreans broke off the engagement and walked down to the road, only to find they had been duped. Surrendering as they did in plain sight, large numbers of their comrades still holed up in the hills elected to also hand themselves over to Colonel Clainos's men. The final tally of North Koreans taken prisoner by Clainos that evening came to 1,700 troops and 13 female nurses.

A US Air Force Sikorsky H-5 lands for the medical evacuation of wounded troops. (Photo USAF)

At 7.45 p.m., Colonel Clainos raised 3RAR by radio to inform the Australians of his approach, with vehicle lights blazing and North Korean PoWs under escort.

At around 11 p.m., the 1/7th Cav arrived at the 3RAR roadblock, where Clainos reputedly heard an Australian soldier mutter in a typical Antipodean drawl: 'Now what do you make of this? Here we are all set for a coordinated attack in the morning, and the bloody Yanks come in at midnight from the north, with their lights burning, and bringing the whole damned North Korean Army as prisoners.'

This was an understandable impression, as the column, stretched out over 20 miles, in south–north order, was made up of the US 24th Infantry Division, North Korean PoWs, two companies of 1/Argylls, North Korean PoWs, the rest of 1/Argylls, North Korean PoWs, 3RAR, North Korean PoWs and finally the 1/7th Cav. The 7th Cavalry had covered 43 miles that day.

Final preparations were now being made for the final thrust on P'yŏngyang, an honour claimed by the US 1st Cavalry Division as the 27th British had beaten the US 24th Infantry Division to Sariwŏn.

US Eighth Army intelligence estimated that fewer than 8,000 North Korean troops, the remnants of the KPA 17th and 32nd divisions, defended the North Korean capital.

DOCUMENT ON KOREAN SITUATION ISSUED BY CHINESE COMMUNIST PARTY CENTRAL AUTHORITIES

1. On 3 October the Peiping Municipal Committee of the Chinese Communist Party received a document from the central authorities of the Party analysing the Korean situation. The statement stated that when the North Koreans withdrew from Seoul [when] the Korean war entered a new stage; but that during the initial stage of the campaign the North Korean Army had annihilated 70,000 American and South Korean troops and had liberated 95 percent of Korea.

2. The document makes the following analysis of the situation:
   a. The war will be a long one, from which the Americans will not be able to extricate themselves.
   b. The North Korean Army is not crushed, but remains a huge and powerful force.
   c. All American forces in the Far East are now committed. Neither the United States nor other United Nations countries involved in the war can send more troops to Korea; defeat is therefore inevitable.
   d. All Koreans are united behind KIM Il-sung.
   e. Fighting will become fiercer, and the North Koreans may withdraw from Pyongyang just as the People's Liberation Army withdrew from Yenan.
   f. It is predicted that the North Koreans with the sympathy and support of all peace loving people, particularly the people of China, will no doubt win final victory.

Comment

It is significant that this document follows the Communist line as presented to the people in the press. It shows no indication that the Chinese Communist leaders are trying to whip up support for covert armed intervention in Korea. On the contrary, it appears to be an explanation to the Party rank and file that intervention is not necessary, and may well be evidence that as of 3 October the Chinese Communists did not plan to intervene in Korea.

Declassified CIA Secret Information Report, 17 October 1950

With the US I Corps approaching from the south and four South Korean divisions from the south and south-east, it was considered very likely that the main force that constituted the city's defence would withdraw northward across the Ch'ŏngch'ŏn River. General MacArthur's designs of the US X Corps completing a flanking operation on P'yŏngyang

The South Koreans are greeted by waving crowds as they advance deeper into North Korea.

from the east had failed to materialize. While the corps' combat elements languished helplessly off Wŏnsan and at Pusan harbour, the determined South Korean forces had at breath-taking pace penetrated deeply into northern and central North Korea. The ROKA 1st Infantry Division, 15 miles to the south-east of P'yŏngyang, were, at the end of 17 October, the closest of all UN forces. On its right flank the ROKA 7th Infantry Division was closing in from the east, while the ROKA 8th Infantry Division was close to Yangdŏk in the central mountains, poised to cut the Wŏnsan–P'yŏngyang lateral road towards the capital. Having struck west from Wŏnsan two days earlier, the ROKA 6th Infantry Division was within 50 air miles of the capital.

As dawn broke on 18 October, General Gay issued orders for the US 7th Cavalry—the farthest north—to recommence the march on P'yŏngyang. At 6.30 a.m., the 3RAR vehicle column left Sariwŏn for Hwangju to release the 3/7th Cav for its northward move. Major R. A. Gordon's A Company, with Shermans from D Company, US 89th Tank Battalion, led the Australian column on to Hwangju in an uneventful move. Upon their arrival, General Gay ordered 3RAR to proceed to the mining town and port of Kyŏmip'o on the Taedong River, 15 miles north-west of Hwangju. However, as the leading company reached Kyŏmip'o, fresh orders were received for the battalion to proceed to P'yŏngyang instead, following a northward route via the village of Samgap'o. The unhappy Australians protested that the first directive, amended due to a lack of enemy resistance, deprived them of the honour of being the first of the UN forces to enter P'yŏngyang.

SCHOOL COLLECTION REFUSED

Comforts Plan For 'Diehards'
Permission to arrange a collection among children of Roe Green Junior School, Princes-avenue. Kingsbury, to provide comforts for men of the Middlesex Regiment serving in Korea has been refused by Wembley Education Committee. The committee resolved that while appreciating this was a worthy object, it was not possible to vary the general ruling that collections should not be made in schools.

The request to make the collection came from the headmaster, Mr. G. A. Johnson. During the war the school collected in aid of men of the 2nd Battalion of the Middlesex Regiment—before Dunkirk the children gave enough to send 18,000 cigarettes—and contributed money for the battalion's welfare fund. The school also sent books and gift parcels to sailors on H.M.S. Glen Kidston.

Another worthy cause which used to be supported by Roe Green schoolchildren, before the ban on collections in schools was introduced, was Dr. Barnardo's Homes, and the school subscribed enough to pay for the maintenance of a girl there.

Harrow Observer, 19 October 1950

Covering 33 miles, as 3RAR approached Samgap'o, A Company came under sniper fire. The enemy action was quickly silenced by 90mm high-explosive fire from the tanks and Browning .50-calibre machine-gun fire. A Company conducted a sweep through the village to high ground 500 yards to the north. Five North Koreans were killed and three captured. The Australians did not sustain any casualties and battalion headquarters was established in Samgap'o for the night.

That morning, the remainder of the British 27th had followed 3RAR out of Sariwŏn, moving on P'yŏngyang on the division's left flank. The US 8th Cavalry remained to hold the town. Not long after jumping off, Brigadier Coad's men became entangled in a massive traffic jam at a blown bridge, where the US 5th and 7th cavalry regiments were jostling for priority crossing. Finally, all traffic had to yield to the 7th Cavalry, followed by the 5th. The British 27th, less 3RAR, were ordered off the road and obliged to harbour a short distance south of Hwangju. Late that evening, Brigadier Coad received orders that his brigade had been given a priority window to cross the river between 6 a.m. and 9 a.m. the following morning.

Meanwhile, to the north the US 7th Cavalry had been making good progress on its drive toward the North Korean capital city. However, as the assault battalion, the 3/7th Cav, approached the small town of Hŭkkyo-ri, it started taking heavy, high-velocity and 120mm mortar fire from high ground to the front. An estimated 800 North Koreans, firmly entrenched in well-prepared defensive positions, brought regimental commander Colonel James K. Woolnough's advance to an abrupt halt.

Whilst the Americans had significant support in the form of twenty tanks of C Company, US 70th Tank Battalion, the road ahead had been heavily mined. They also had to contend with four hull-down T-34 tanks. During the fighting, enemy small-arms fire downed an F-51 Mustang fighter.

Appraising the situation from an apple orchard next to the road, corps commander General Milburn was joined by General Gay, who expressed to his commander his dissatisfaction with the lack of progress. The other two battalions were ordered to start flanking movements on the enemy position. In spite of protests from some of the junior officers who felt that such a manoeuvre was pointless as the North Korean position was close to being taken, Colonel Woolnough had already committed the 1/7th Cav and 2/7th Cav battalions. It turned out to be an exercise in futility, taking all night to accomplish, only to find at first light that the North Koreans had scarpered in the darkness.

On the morning of 19 October, General Gay issued orders for the US 5th Cavalry, commanded by Colonel Marcel G. Crombez, to pass through the 7th Cavalry to take up the advance on P'yŏngyang. But the regiment was still so stretched out on the mountainous

P-51 Mustangs from the US Air Force 8th Fighter Bomber Group at Kimp'o Airfield. (Photo Lieutenant Colonel Harvey W. Gipple)

Near P'yŏngyang the food and cigarette shortage became unbearable. A typical meal at the time was a slice of Spam and a half canteen-cup of grapefruit juice—once a day. We stripped the countryside bare in our search to find anything edible. There is a popular belief, circulated mainly by Hollywood, that combat soldiers talk about nothing but sex. This is totally false.

In fact, as we grew hungrier and hungrier, we talked of nothing but food. We had reveries about food in the day and dreams about food at night. It obsessed us. We titillated each other dreaming up meals we would prepare if we got home.

The craving for cigarettes was partially satisfied by smoking dried leaves wrapped in C-ration toilet paper. The irony of it all, as in every war, is that just a few miles behind the front, rear-echelon troops have all the food and cigarettes they could possibly want.

Another problem was the weather, which grew colder. We still had not been issued winter uniforms. I will never forget my disgust with Lieutenant Geer when he ordered me to remove a fur cap I had taken off a dead North Korean soldier. He told me it was unsoldierly, that I would have to be satisfied with my fatigue cap and helmet.

Private James Cardinal, I Company, US 5th Cavalry[*]

---

[*] Donald Knox, *The Korean War, Pusan to Chosin: An Oral History* (Harcourt Brace & Co., Orlando, 1985).

secondary road from Sŏhŭng that it would be close to midnight before Crombez had assembled all his troops in Hwangju.

Having jumped off from Samgap'o at 6.30 a.m., 3RAR's advance was severely restricted by rain and the atrocious condition of the roads. The battalion's Pioneer Platoon, under Captain S. W. Ness, and aided by US Army engineers, fought an uphill battle to make the road serviceable.

At 11 a.m., the leading Sherman tanks of Major W. F. Brown's D Company, US 89th Tank Battalion, took four armour-piercing shells and machine-gun fire from enemy tanks. After one tank burning out, the American armour moved forward to find another well-concealed T-34 and an SU-76 self-propelled gun. Both had run out of fuel and been abandoned. The enemy vehicles were destroyed by tank fire before the battalion established its headquarters at Paeng-ni at 1 p.m.

By this time, the 27th British HQ and 1/Middlesex had been rerouted back to Hwangju, and from there westward. The 1/Argylls was trailing 3RAR. Swinging west again at Chunghwa, the brigade linked up with 3RAR, at which point the unit harboured for the

A Soviet 76mm self-propelled gun.

night in persistent torrential rain that was bitterly cold. The brigade had no radio contact with the US 1st Infantry Division, so were in the dark as to the state of play at P'yŏngyang. Brigadier Coad felt isolated, feeling that he would have to make his own way to the capital, oblivious to what awaited him and his men.

At 10 a.m. on 20 October, Brigadier Coad jumped off as best he could on a 'road' that was barely passable, 1/Middlesex leading the way. Without seeing any sign of the enemy, five hours later 1/Middlesex entered P'yŏngyang from the south-west. It was only at this stage that Brigadier Coad found out that the US 5th Cavalry had taken the city, closely followed by the rest of the US 1st Cavalry Division, while the ROKA 1st Infantry Division had secured the northern parts. At this time, 3RAR had moved to Yonge-ri, 3 miles from the city's south-western outskirts, where the decision was made to bivouac for the night.

Lieutenant Colonel Paul Clifford had led the 2/5th Cav out from Hwangju at 5 a.m. Arriving at the final stages of a North Korean counterattack on the US 7th Cavalry at Hŭkkyo-ri, a bazooka team with the 2/5th Cav knocked out three enemy T-34s.

Passing through the US 7th Cavalry, officer commanding F Company, 2/5th Cav, Lieutenant James H. Bell, led his men and the rest of the US 5th Cavalry toward P'yŏngyang. Colonel Crombez and a small contingent of command staff fell in behind F Company to maintain an optimum rate of advance. Flights of Lockheed P-80 Shooting Stars provided air support.

An hour before noon, Lieutenant Bell reached the Mujin, a small tributary of the Taedong River which flows through P'yŏngyang. After neutralizing a North Korean emplacement of three anti-tank guns, F Company crossed the Mujin and entered the south-eastern fringes of the capital. The unit then crossed a railway bridge onto an island in the middle of the Taedong.

To the rear of F Company, Captain Norman Allen's I Company, 3/5th Cav, approached a dyke just before the railway bridge across the Taedong. Following an uneventful advance, Captain Allen dismounted from his jeep at the head of his company to check the final short distance alongside the dyke and onto the bridge. No sooner had he left his vehicle when, according to him:

> I looked into the eyes of a North Korean soldier. He turned to run and I dropped him. Excited about getting out of that one and of hitting the sonovabitch, I failed to notice an enemy machine gun off to my right along the riverbank. It was only when I turned to wave the lead platoon forward that from the corner of my eye caught the gun's movement as it shifted toward me. By this time I was a little ways down the reverse slope of the dike and didn't know what to do. I froze. The machine gun suddenly swung away from me and engaged another target, then moved back to me. Just then M Company's CO, a redhead Texan named Walt Watts, charged down into them, waving his .45. Swinging left and right, hitting here, banging there, he captured the entire enemy crew without firing a shot. For more than an hour Captain Watts marched these North Koreans up and down the road until I'm sure the entire regiment saw them. (He received a Silver Star for the episode—deserved it too, for he had surely saved my ass.)[*]

After positioning supporting armour, machine guns and mortars along the river's edge to provide cover, I Company started across the railway bridge to relieve F Company on the island. Upon reaching the island, the North Koreans blew up a span that supported the bridge from the island to their side of the river. F Company now made their way back to the airfield on the south bank.

At this time, E and G companies, 2/5th Cav, were nearing the adjacent highway bridge, the only bridge across the Taedong still intact. As they approached, however, the North Koreans blew the centre span.

By the end of the day, all of P'yŏngyang south of the Taedong had been secured by the 1st and 3rd battalions of the US 5th Cavalry. The Americans would have a 'cold and wet and dark' night under constant harassment from North Korean artillery and small-arms fire. During the night, commanding officer of the 3/5th Cav, Colonel Edgar J. Treacy, arrived on the Taedong island where I Company was bivouacked, to inform Captain Allen that his unit were to cross the river at first light the next morning. Groups from 8th Engineers would bring boats to the island for the crossing.

---

[*] Ibid.

North Koreans fleeing P'yŏngyang clamber over a damaged bridge spanning the Taedong River, Pyongyang, October 1950. (Photo Sergeant D. Helms)

Torrents of rain fell as I Company's 3rd squad moved to the south of the island, with a machine gun, to guide the engineers to the secured position. The GIs were miserably cold, soaked and very hungry—many had forgotten when they last had a hot meal.

In what seemed like an eternity, the engineers, under a green-horn Westpoint graduate, delivered five boats—and one paddle. To exacerbate Captain Allen's problems further, he had received no information about the speed that the river was flowing at or what its width was. Where the Taedong flows through P'yŏngyang, it is between 400 and 500 yards wide.

While Captain Allen tried to find answers to this conundrum, elsewhere on the island Lieutenant Lester Blevins was having an acrimonious exchange of words with division artillery on the south bank who insisted on positioning their 155mm howitzers in the river dyke, a position that the 3/5th Cav had earmarked for the placement of its M2 4.2-inch mortars and the ubiquitous 'Four-Deuce' or 'Goon Gun'. Despite warnings about the consequences of dropping shells short, the gunners were adamant that it was their prerogative to decide where and how to employ their hardware.

As the sky started to grey on the morning of 20 October, and the first wave, 1st Platoon, I Company, prepared to launch their boats for the crossing, Captain Allen's misgivings became a reality when a short round fell on his command post. Several men were wounded, including Lieutenant Blevins. Rushing up to the blast site, Captain Allen found the lieutenant spread-eagled on his back:

> He'd been hit in the groin. Top Mitchell pointed to a cordlike thing that stretched out from him about twenty feet. 'What'n hell's that?' Top whispered, 'Testicles.' I had never seen anything like that. Top said, 'I'll cut it off up close.' 'Hell no,' I said, 'let's roll the stuff up and stick it in his crotch bandage. Let some doctor make that decision."

As the engineers worked on getting the first detachment across, division artillery pounded the north bank, while supporting fire from 2/5th Cav concentrated their aim on the embankment skyline. Fortuitously, the strong current swept the rubber assault boats 100 yards past the intended landing stage at the base of the railway bridge—at least one North Korean machine-gun nest protected that point. As the boats beached on the north bank, a severe firefight erupted, the sounds of men shouting carrying across to the island. At this, frantic efforts were made to stop the American artillery from firing for fear of killing the American troops now scrambling onto the north bank. The howitzers finally fell silent, but not before a shell disabled one of the returning boats.

The crossing slowed even more, the situation aggravated by engineers personnel employing delaying tactics, understandably petrified of venturing across the river once more. As if to quantify their fears, one of the boats arrived back at the island carrying several dead bodies in sloshing bloody water.

The second wave—2nd Platoon—came under heavy fire from the north bank during the crossing. At the landing area, the shore extended for 100 feet before ending against a 15-feet-high dyke with a concrete bunker at its base. A grenade was lobbed into the bunker to ensure the elimination of any possible threat.

The I Company troops, accompanied by South Korean KATUSA (Korean Augmentation to the United States Army) soldiers, scaled the dyke to look on the smoke-covered North Korean capital for the first time. The men immediately opened fire on scores of KPA troops seen running in between buildings in some confusion.

The 3rd Platoon crossed next, the boat occupants using rifle butts and their hands to paddle against the strong current. About halfway across, a 'redheaded kid' made the mistake of standing up. He took several hits, tumbled into the river and was swept away never to be seen again. I Company was to lose four men that day.

---

* Ibid.

AGES OF BRITISH SOLDIERS IN KOREA

House of Commons debate, 19 September 1950

Mr [Captain] Albert Blackburn [MP]: How many troops under the age of 20 are now serving in Korea?

Mr Evelyn Strachey [Secretary of State for War]: It would be very difficult to obtain this information for him, and I am not willing to put on to Far Eastern Command the burden of doing that at the moment. On the broader question, I must repeat what I said in the Debate—that what we have established is the rule that no soldier under 19 years of age, whether National Service man or Regular, will serve in Korea.

Blackburn: Does the Secretary of State for War really mean to say that he has no idea, on which he could form an estimate, about how many troops out of the 2,000 in Korea are under the age of 20?

Mr Strachey: The information could be obtained from Far Eastern Command but, for the reasons I have given, I do not intend to seek it.

Mr Reader Harris [MP]: Are there no records in this country which would give the information?

Strachey: It would entail the verification by Far Eastern Command of all these individuals and the information being sent back here. At this moment, when the pressure on the Far Eastern Command is very great, we do not intend to put this greater burden upon them.

Mr William Teeling [MP]: Are we to understand that all these young men under 20 are sent out from this country without any record being kept here?

Strachey: Their records are at the Headquarters of Far Eastern Command in Singapore.

Mr David Renton [MP]: Is the right hon. Gentleman aware that this information could be obtained in the case of each company by an intelligent N.C.O. within a few minutes?

Mr Blackburn: On a point of order. In view of the nature of the reply, which appears to me to be discourteous to the House of Commons, I propose to raise this matter at the earliest possible opportunity.

Hansard, 19 September 1950

By 9.30 a.m., I Company had completed the hazardous crossing and had established a 700-yard beachhead along the river dyke, centred on the railway bridge. Captain Allen now assembled his company and pushed into the city's housing. The house-to-house

Taedong River, 1949.

sweep encountered terrified old men, women and children who had been fed so much anti-American propaganda that they were convinced they would be killed. However, chewing gum, chocolates and cigarettes rapidly dispelled their fears.

In the northward drive along the city streets, the soldiers had to contend with sporadic sniper, automatic and anti-tank fire from fleeing North Koreans showing little more than token resistance to the imminent fall of their capital. By 2.30 p.m., the 3/5th Cav had secured their objective sector and had established communications with British Commonwealth and South Korean forces in the city. The US 1st Cavalry Division's arrival at P'yŏngyang coincided with the entry into the city, along the Sibyŏn-ni road, of the ROKA 1st Infantry Division to the north-east of the Americans.

As night fell on 18 October, the South Koreans had found themselves only 8 miles from the capital, while the American cavalry still had 30 miles to cover to reach their objective. But the race to P'yŏngyang was not yet a foregone conclusion.

The ROKA 1st Infantry Division had encountered considerably stronger North Korean opposition on a road densely planted with both anti-tank and anti-personnel mines. Division commander General Paik pushed his troops throughout the hours of darkness, before destroying a powerful North Korean defensive position two hours before sunrise. The South Koreans could only advance 2 miles. Near the city of Kojo-dong, General Paik again ran into a well-fortified enemy position that raked his leading troops with automatic fire. While Paik launched an attack from the front, tanks from C Company, 6th Tank Battalion, enveloped both enemy flanks. The 300-strong North Korean stronghold quickly collapsed as tanks clanked over machine guns and enemy soldiers while destroying self-propelled guns.

General Paik had reported further minefields beyond this point, but troops of the ROKA 2nd Battalion, 12th Regiment (ROKA 2/12th) sped ahead relentlessly, reaching the Taedong south bank north-east of the highway bridge a little before 11 a.m. He would report that his C Company tanks had entered the capital's southern boundary at 12.45 p.m.

Tanks of D Company, followed on the same road, entering the city before swinging north toward the airfield, which, together with elements of the ROKA 11th Regiment, was taken at 2.40 p.m.

When the US 2/5th Cav had their designated access road across the Taedong destroyed, Colonel Crombez continued along the south bank in a north-easterly direction, looking for a place to ford the river. A few miles upriver, Crombez came up to a stage where the 15th Regiment, ROKA 1st Infantry Division, had already crossed, thanks to General Paik's knowledge of the area as a native of P'yŏngyang. Also coming in from the east, the 8th Regiment, ROKA 7th Infantry Division, took north P'yŏngyang.

The following day—20 October—General Paik took the administrative heart of the city with relative ease. Despite the fact that the city centre had been extensively fortified,

A North Korean fuel truck explodes after being strafed by an F-51 Mustang. (Photo USAF)

the North Koreans had no fight left in them, electing to abandon their weapons and evacuate their defences. At 10 a.m., Paik declared the North Korean capital secure. By noon, assault boats had ferried the US 3/5th Cav and the US 3/7th Cav across the Taedong.

Task Force Indianhead, named for the shoulder patch of the US 2nd Infantry Division, had accompanied the leading elements of the US 1st Cavalry Division into P'yŏngyang. Commanded by Lieutenant Colonel Ralph L. Foster, Major General Laurence B. Keiser's Assistant Chief of Staff, Intelligence (G-2), the task force was centred on K Company, US 38th Infantry Regiment, and included tanks from C Company, US 72nd Medium Tank Battalion, motorized weapons of the US Anti-aircraft Battalion, engineer demolition teams and counterintelligence troops. Colonel Foster was able to achieve nearly all of his objectives on the first day of occupation, seizing large volumes of intelligence-rich political and military documents that were immediately airlifted to the Far East Command headquarters in Tokyo.

Responsible for order and security in the city, General Gay established his division headquarters at the North Korean Military Academy on the Chinnamp'o road to the coast, 10 miles south-west of the capital. A few days later, Gay appointed Colonel Crombez, who possessed considerable knowledge of North Korea and its people, as Civil Assistance Officer. Colonel Harold K. Johnson took over as commander of the US 5th Cavalry.

General Gay's priority was the disposition of his division units. The US 5th Cavalry would be responsible for security in the southern part of the city, the US 8th Cavalry in the northern part, and the US 7th Cavalry, Chinnamp'o—35 miles from P'yŏngyang—after having taken the port in a night assault on 22 October.

On 24 October, the misery and near failure of the Pusan Perimeter indelibly etched on his mind, General Walton H. Walker moved into North Korean leader Kim Il-sung's seat of power to make the unscathed building his own US Eighth Army Headquarters.

The day after the fall of the North Korean capital, General MacArthur flew into the P'yŏngyang airfield from Japan for a fleeting visit. After a brief conference with General Walker and FEAF commander General George E. Stratemeyer, he reviewed what was left of F Company, US 2/5th Cav, under Lieutenant James H. Bell, the first American unit to enter the capital. Of the original F Company strength that had arrived in Korea three months earlier, only five had survived, of whom only two were not wounded.

5. ATTACK OF THE RAKKASANS

'Was there any meaning to life or to war, that two men should sit together and jump within seconds of each other and yet never meet on the ground below?'

Rifleman D. K. Webster, 506th Regiment, US 101st Airborne Division[*]

For General Douglas MacArthur the capture of P'yŏngyang was, especially following so rapidly on the successes of the Inch'ŏn landings, a major strategic victory. The US Eighth Army had broken the Pusan siege and crossed the 38th Parallel, while on the east coast, the US X Corps had landed to join the ROKA I Corps to complete a hammer and anvil tactic to entrap the ever-retiring North Korean military and political machinery.

However, General MacArthur was ever mindful of the 27 September order from the JCS in Washington to employ all resources available to him to completely annihilate the Korean People's Army north of the 38th Parallel: air, ground and amphibious. With the South Koreans continuing their brisk advance north of Wŏnsan, MacArthur made the decision to capitalize on the US Eighth Army's successes in the centre and west of North Korea to entrap enemy strongholds north of P'yŏngyang and then to strike for the Manchurian border.

Accordingly, on 17 October, MacArthur had issued United Nations Command Operations Order No. 4, calling for an airdrop ahead of North Korean forces north of Korea, while the US I Corps completed the entrapment from the south.

The US 187th Airborne 'Rakkasans' Infantry Regiment, based at the time at the Kimp'o Airfield as General Headquarters reserve after having assisted the US X Corps to clear the Han River south bank when Seoul was taken, was selected to provide the airborne element. The unit had adopted the sobriquet 'Rakkasans' for the word a Japanese translator had concocted for airborne soldiers, which literally translated as 'falling down umbrella men'.

Activated on 25 February 1943 as the two-battalion US 187th Glider Infantry Regiment, the men underwent parachute and glider training at Camp Mackall and Camp Polk before entering the Pacific theatre on active service in May 1944. Attached to the US 11th Airborne Division, in May 1945, while preparing for the Allied invasion of Japan—Operation Downfall—a third battalion was activated and the 187th redesignated a para-glider regiment. In August, the regiment took on occupation duty on Okinawa, before returning to the United States in April the following year.

---

[*] David Kenyon Webster, *Parachute Infantry: An American Paratrooper's Memoir of D-Day and the Fall of the Third Reich.* (Louisiana State University Press, 1994).

Members of the 187th ARCT kitting up for a jump. (Photo NARA)

In June 1949, the unit was retitled the US 187th Airborne Infantry Regiment (US 187th), before being selected as an airborne regimental combat team (ARCT) for deployment to Korea under the command of Colonel Frank S. Bowen. General Order 34 (Confidential) Headquarters 11th Airborne Division, augmented the ARCT strength with the US 674th Airborne FAB (105mm), A Battery, US 88th Airborne Anti-aircraft Artillery Battalion and A Company, US 127th Airborne Engineer Battalion.

The objective was identified and fixed along the Sukch'ŏn–Sunch'ŏn axis, some 30 miles north of P'yongyang. From the city, two roads diverge in the form of a V northward, each roughly in parallel with a rail line.

The UN Command was by this time confident that no organized North Korean units remained north of the 38th Parallel, but only disjointed and scattered bodies of soldiers. It would be these retreating remnants of the Pusan offensive that would offer the US Eighth Army any form of resistance. Heavy equipment and armour had been abandoned along all their routes of escape.

It was perceived that the North Koreans' mission was to mount a limited defence of Sukch'ŏn and Sunch'ŏn so as to keep the east coast routes open to the north, and to

RUSSIANS FIGHT TO SACK LIE

From Herald Reporter, Lake Success, Friday.
The battle over the Secretary-Generalship of the United Nations continued today behind the closed doors of the Security Council, with the Russians using every device to get rid of Trygve Lie, whose five-year term ends in February. This is the second time since the war the Big Powers have engaged in backstairs intrigue over the job, one of the biggest in the world, and for the second time Norwegian Trygve Lie is at the centre of it. His election in 1946 on the Security Council's nomination was an East-West compromise.

Final Crime
The United States and other countries suggest his term should extended for two or three years, but Vishinsky and Malik have been conducting a savage campaign against the proposal. His final crime in Russian eyes was calling together the Security Council to act on Korea. Now the Russians seem ready to accept 'anybody but Lie.' First they tried to get a Pole nominated. Then they said they would settle for a Latin-American or Asian delegate. Last night they tried to rope in Philippine Foreign Minister Romulo. And today Malik was hinting that they would take American delegate Warren Austin.

Mr. Malik told reporters today that he has had a meeting with John Foster Dulles.

Double Faced
'Dulles told me,' he said, 'that Mr. Lie had followed a double-faced policy, but that the United States had made too heavy commitments to drop him now.' But Mr. Dulles immediately issued a denial. He said: 'This is another attempt of the Soviet Union to discredit the Secretary General Lie because of the firm stand he has taken in support of United Nations's action in resisting aggression in Korea.'

Daily Herald, 21 October 1950

execute counteroffensives to re-establish a corridor to the west coast. The force comprised an amalgam of the 2,500-strong KPA 239th Regiment plus 3,500 troops from a miscellany of small units. The force was equipped with 82mm and 120mm mortars, 40mm guns, various artillery pieces, recoilless rifles, light machine guns and 14.5mm anti-tank rifles.

To date, no intelligence had been received of any overt Soviet or Chinese troop presence south of the Yalu River. It was known, however, that Beijing had massed 100,000 troops of the People's Liberation Army (PLA) Fourth Field Army on the border, referring to the

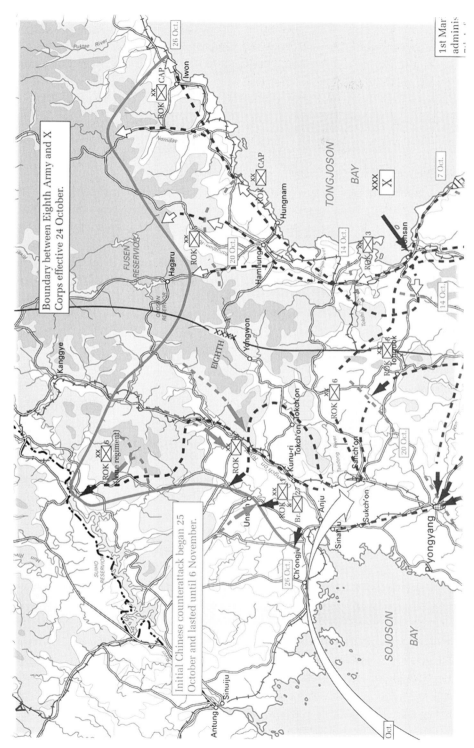

The situation in North Korea from mid-October 1950. (Wikimedia)

body as the Chinese People's Volunteer Army (CPVA) in an apparent attempt to disguise the presence of a standing Chinese army. The army was commanded by the 52-year-old Marshal Peng Dehuai, a veteran of Mao Zedong's Long March and staunch Communist Party of China member.

By 22 October, the US 187th ARCT had a strength of 3,950 combat-experienced men, with available reinforcements of one cavalry battalion, two tank companies and one reinforced infantry brigade. After arriving at Kimp'o Airfield, the 187th ARTC was tasked with clearing the Kimp'o Peninsula of the KPA 107th Security Regiment, a mission in which they were extremely successful.

Deemed to be combat fit, the unit was armed and equipped with 105mm howitzers, 90mm anti-tank guns, 25mm recoilless rifles, .30-calibre machine guns, flame throwers, 4.2-inch mortars, M-1 rifles, .45 calibre pistols, Browning automatic rifles (BARs), light machine guns and 60mm mortars.

On 17 October, Colonel Bowen briefed his regimental officers on the mission and objectives. After seizing and securing the Sukch'ŏn–Sunch'ŏn area, enemy main supply routes (MSR) and lines of communication (LOC) were to be disrupted to block enemy withdrawal northward and to prevent supplies from reaching stranded enemy troops to the south. High-ranking North Korean military and civilian personnel were to be flushed out and captured. Upon the satisfactory completion of these primary missions, raids were to be conducted to liberate American and South Korean PoWs.

The objective for the 2nd Battalion, US 187th ARCT (2/187th), was to airdrop on Drop Zone (DZ) Easy, centred on Sunch'ŏn. To the west, the 1st and 3rd battalions (1/187th and 3/187th) were to drop on DZ William at Sukch'ŏn. The two objectives would be cleared of enemy forces and secured, followed by the establishment of roadblocks to prevent enemy troops from escaping and to disrupt enemy channels of supply and communication.

Initially scheduled for 21 October, D-Day for the airborne strike was brought forward a day as a result of the speed with which the US Eighth Army had advanced from the 38th Parallel. Despite misgivings in the US Combat Cargo Command about the suitability of Kimp'o as the staging point, about half the US 2348th Quartermaster Air Supply and Packaging Company was airlifted from the Ashiya Air Force Base (AFB) in Japan to Kimp'o to prepare for the attack.

The US Far East Air Force (FEAF) Combat Cargo Command, under Major General William H. Tunner, at the time comprised the 1st, 61st, 314th and 315th troop carrier groups (TCGs) and the 374th, 403rd, 437th and 483rd troop carrier wings (TCWs). On 18 October—D-Day-2—General Tunner cancelled all operational transport commitments of the US 314th TCG Fairchild C-119 Flying Boxcars and of the 21st Troop Carrier Squadron's Douglas C-47 Skytrains, for thorough maintenance.

US Fifth Air Force aircraft were moved from Kimp'o to provide the necessary room demanded of the huge airborne task force. However, fighters from the air force would be deployed to soften up the US 187th's objectives and to provide escorts for the troop

A Fairchild C-119 Flying Boxcar of the 403rd Troop Carrier Wing. (Photo NARA)

carriers. Elements of the US 6147th Tactical Air Control Group, known as the 'Mosquitoes', were to provide a large-scale, effective forward air control (FAC) system that included both airborne and ground-based FACs.

In a series of combat firsts, the Sukch'ŏn–Sunch'ŏn airborne assault was the first time that heavy equipment was para-dropped in combat, and the first use of C-119 transports for a combat parachute operation. On 20 October and the days following, about 4,000 troops—2,860 on D-Day—12 105mm howitzers, 39 jeeps and trailers, 4 40mm anti-aircraft artillery guns, 4 three-quarter-ton trucks, and 584 tons of ammunition, fuel, water, rations and other supplies were dropped into the two drop zones.

On 19 October—D-Day-1—the US 187th completed packing for the next day's assault. Kit bags and sleeping bags were loaded on to trucks for overland shipment to the secured drop zones. After ammunition and rations issue, individual companies held troops briefings, followed that evening by a final briefing for pilots and jumpmasters in one of the hangars.

Reveille was at 2 a.m. on 20 October and the paratroopers formed into ordered twenty-three-man sticks and shuttled to the airfield. Following two three-hour delays in the scheduled jump-off time, largely due to torrential rain, the order to 'chute-up' was finally issued at 10.30 a.m.

It quickly became evident, however, that in many cases the air transports would exceed the prescribed maximum payload of 15,500 lb. Typically, a C-119 carried forty-six paratroopers (two sticks), fifteen monorail bundles and four door bundles. Some of the men

Members of the 187th ARCT crammed into the hold of a C-119 Boxcar. (Photo NARA)

were forced to sit on the floor for lack of space. Each combatant, in addition to his main and reserve parachutes, carried a light pack, water, rations, ammunition, a .45-calibre pistol and a carbine or M-1 rifle. Some men carried extra Griswold containers filled with small-arms or light mortar ammunition. The container was equipped with a snap hook for attachment to the parachute harness. Worn diagonally across the chest, and tucked under the reserve parachute, the container was closed with a steel rod, which allowed the container to be instantly opened much like the ripcord on a parachute pack.

Early that afternoon, US Fifth Air Force fighters and light bombers conducted seek-and-destroy sorties against North Korean positions in the two drop zones.

Under F-51 Mustang escort, at noon the airlift fleet of seventy-three C-119s of the US 314th TCG, commanded by Colonel E. W. Hampton from Ashiya AFB, Kyushu, Japan, and forty C-47s of the 21st Troop Carrier Squadron, US 374th TCW, from Brady AFB, Kyushu, ferrying 2,860 paratroopers and 300 tons of equipment and supplies, took off from Kimp'o, and in tight formation, swung out over the Yellow Sea. The regiment command post flew in aircraft Nos 1 and 20, while General Tunner flew alongside the formation. General MacArthur was in close observation in his personal aircraft.

KNOW YOUR ENEMY

Of the many professional sins of which Douglas MacArthur was guilty in that moment, including hubris and vanity, none was greater than his complete underestimation of the enemy.

As Bruce Cumings, a historian of the Korean War, noted, Asians in MacArthur's mind were 'obedient, dutiful, childlike, and quick to follow resolute leadership.' MacArthur's China had not been touched by the Communist revolution. He seemed not to care how and why Mao had come to power, and had little interest in the forces that the revolution had unleashed. He seemed to believe that the Communists' victory in the civil war had little larger meaning. As a military force the Communists were 'grossly overrated,' he had told congressional representatives in September 1949, a month before Mao proclaimed his government. The way to beat them, he had said at the time, was to hit them 'where they are weakest, namely in the air and on the sea.' All you had to do, he added, was place '500 fighter planes, under the command of some old war horse similar to ("Flying Tigers" commander) General Chennault.' MacArthur had used his airpower skilfully in his campaign in the Pacific against the Japanese, as a kind of long-distance artillery, and he seemed to believe that he would be able to use it much the same way against the Chinese.

David Halberstam, 'MacArthur's Grand Delusion' in *Hive*, October 2007

Flying north along the coast, at 1.55 p.m. the formation turned to the east, fixing on a base-leg approach to the drop zones at Sukch'ŏn and Sunch'ŏn. At 1.57 p.m., at eight minutes from target, doors were opened and door bundles, held in place by the first man in each stick, were pushed out. At four minutes out, the red light came on and the troops ordered to 'stand up and hook up'. Final checks were conducted while watching US fighters strafing the drop zones. Within a minute the green light came on and 1,470 paratroopers and 74 tons of equipment disgorged from the first two serials. Upon hitting the ground, the leading elements rapidly formed into platoon units to secure high ground commanding the drop zones.

The US 1/187th, together with headquarters and engineering, medical and services support staff and equipment, and the attached FAC party debouched from seventeen C-119s. On the ground, A and B companies assembled and struck to the north to secure Hill 104 overlooking the village of Mail-ri. To the north-east of Sukch'ŏn, airstrikes were called in to target an estimated 1,800 North Koreans in and to the north of the town. C Company followed, employing mortar fire to take Hill 97, before reverting to reserve status. At 3.50 p.m., the battalion command post was set up.

Waiting for the green light. (Photo NARA)

After a forty-five-minute delay caused by enemy fire in Sukch'ŏn, A Company, US 127th Engineer Battalion, moved north behind B Company, US 1/187th, arriving at Songnani-ni at 3.30 p.m. By 9.30 p.m., the engineers had joined B Company near Poegun-san, having captured thirty-one North Koreans and killed five on their way via Namil-li.

Shortly after landing, the US 187th ARCT assembled on the Ch'oeryŏng River where, by 4 p.m., the regiment command post was established.

Commander of the US 647th FAB, Lieutenant Colonel Harry F. Lambert, had jumped from the first transport with Colonel Bowen. Addressing the dispositions of A Battery (Captain Morton) and C Battery (First Lieutenant Baker), Lambert established an observation post on Hill 97. At 2.15 p.m., 7 105mm howitzers, 7 jeeps and 1,125 shells were airdropped for the battalion. A C Battery howitzer was destroyed on impact with the ground when its parachute failed to open. Forty-five minutes later, C Battery had two howitzers in position on the drop zone, ready to fire. By 3.40 p.m., A Battery had four howitzers in position and registered. On the first day of the operation, the two batteries executed six missions, firing a total of sixty shells. By the end of the day, the battalion had 500 shells in stock.

C-119 Boxcars from the 315th Troop Carrier Group drop 187th ARCT paratroopers. (Photo USAF)

The US 3/187th, commanded by Lieutenant Delbert E. Munson, followed the 1/187th into Drop Zone William on serials six and seven. By 5 p.m., the battalion was dug in on commanding ground 3,000 yards south of Sukch'ŏn, with orders to establish a roadblock and be ready to move south to P'yŏngyang. I and K companies were in defensive positions in the left and right half of the battalion respectively, with the latter setting up a roadblock on the Sukch'ŏn–P'yŏngyang road. L Company was held in reserve. So far, the 2/187th had not sustained any casualties. In turn, it had captured forty-two and killed five enemy soldiers. Having been positioned on the rail line south of Sukch'ŏn, A Company, US 127th Engineer Battalion, attached to the 3/187th, ambushed an estimated eighty North Korean soldiers, killing six.

At 2.20 p.m., the US 2/187th dropped into Drop Zone Easy at Sunch'ŏn, accompanied by 2nd platoon, A Company, US 127th Engineer Battalion, a 4.2-inch mortar platoon from Support Company, a 90mm anti-tank section, B Battery, US 647th FAB, the 2nd Pathfinder Team and an FAC party. Although the paratroopers were immediately engaged by the North Koreans, the battalion objectives were successfully attained. E Company took the town of Changsan-ni, before setting up a roadblock on the bridge across the Kŭmch'ŏn River to the south of Sinhung-ni.

F Company mounted an attack on Sunch'ŏn itself, encountering sporadic sniper fire. The battalion command post was established in a hamlet to the south of Chung-ni, while holding G Company in reserve.

The heavy serial drop that came next had limited success. Both quarter-ton trucks were badly damaged and one of the two artillery field pieces written off. Recovering 600 shells from the drop zone, the single howitzer was positioned and registered in 50 minutes, before firing two missions.

Airborne troops board for the second serial drop. (Photo NARA)

At the bridge across the Kŭmch'ŏn south of Sinhung-ni, North Korean fire prevented the men from the US 127th Engineer Battalion from placing explosives to destroy the structure. As a consequence, the engineers were instead assigned to F Company to reconnoitre a railway bridge on the outskirts of Sunch'ŏn. En route, one platoon was mistakenly fired on by elements of the ROKA 6th Infantry Division, but once contact was established the South Koreans broke off without inflicting any damage. That first night was uneventful for the US 187th, even Colonel Bowen's promotion to brigadier general going unnoticed.

Early on the morning of 21 October, Brigadier Coad received orders that his 27th British Commonwealth Brigade had been transferred from the US 1st Cavalry Division to fall under the command of the US 24th Infantry Division. The division had been directed to move north of P'yŏngyang to the MacArthur Line, but the Americans were still so far to the rear that it fell on Brigadier Coad to spearhead the advance with the objective of securing the road and rail bridge across the Ch'ŏngch'ŏn River at Sinanju.

For the 1/Argylls, leading the advance, progress out of the city was slowed down by heavy military traffic. However, once clear, the Scottish battalion covered the 21 miles to Yongju without opposition. The leading company briefly came under small-arms fire as it neared the town, but the North Koreans immediately broke off the engagement when tanks joined the advance. Having established contact with forward elements of the US 187th ARCT in Yongju, Brigadier Coad positioned his brigade for the night in hills to the south of the town. On Coad's right, the ROKA 1st Infantry Division had also jumped off from P'yŏngyang, advancing north-east on the Sunch'ŏn–Anju axis.

The opening paragraph of US 187th ARCT war diary entry for 21 October summed up the operation's status:

> At 0700 hours the 1st and 3rd Battalions continued the attack. However, the enemy still had shown no organized resistance owing to surprise achieved by the drop. The 187th RCT had dropped across one of the enemy's major defensive lines indicated by extensive dug in positions and large quantities of military stores. The night of 20 October 1950 had found the 187th RCT on the strategic offensive and the tactical defensive. Now, the 187th was assuming the tactical offensive.[*]

As the 1/187th resumed its attack on high ground to the north of Sukch'ŏn, only light resistance was encountered as A Company took Hill 142 and B Company Hill 126. This was followed soon after noon by airstrikes on hills 116, 93, 76, and 175 that made up the next ridge line to the north.

---

[*] Maj (P) Phill Pittman et al, *The Battle of Sukchon-Sunchon 20–25 October, 1950.* (Combat Studies Institute, Fort Leavenworth, May 1984).

It was probably during the night hours of October 23–24 that I Company really got smashed on the booze from that warehouse [in P'yŏngyang]. Since some teetotallers and I elected not to drink, we were told to keep an eye on the festivities. We sober guys were surprised at times how otherwise normal men, when loosened by vodka, expressed personal thoughts. In different drinking groups the same kinds of war stories were told, so were thoughts of home and loved ones. On this one night everyone became buddy-buddy, *including* [company commander] Captain Allen!

That night the area around the Russian embassy became a highly dangerous place to be near. Heavy drinking and armed men do not mix. Guys tossed grenades over the wall without knowing whether anyone was on the other side. Small arms were fired. Eventually, the party turned into just plain, unrestricted hell-raising. It must have been something like this in the Old West when a trail gang, after eight weeks of herding longhorn, rode into Dodge. No-one interfered or tried to. As far as I can recall, no one was killed or even injured. The following day I Company had all its excess ammo and hand grenades taken away.

Pfc. Victor Cox, I Company, US 5th Cavalry[*]

[*] Donald Knox, *The Korean War, Pusan to Chosin: An Oral History* (Harcourt Brace & Co., Orlando, 1985).

An hour later, while B Company called in artillery fire on Tojang-ni, battalion commander, Lieutenant Colonel Arthur H. Wilson ordered the forward companies to seize hills 76, 175 and 68, and to dig in on these objectives. On the southern slopes of Hill 76, an estimated seventy-five entrenched North Koreans opened fire on the advancing A Company with rifles and machine guns. From the rear of the hill, 82mm mortars also fired on the Americans, while farther back near Tŭngnyŏng-ni, a high-velocity self-propelled gun gave added weight to the North Korean defences.

As light was beginning to fade, the 1/187th opened a command post at the foot of Hill 76, from where a platoon from reserve Company C was sent out establish contact with a patrol of 2/187th from Sunch'ŏn. This was successfully achieved on the Maenam-ni–Sunch'ŏn road in Drop Zone Easy at 6.30 p.m.

During the hours of darkness, at 2.30 a.m. that same day, a company-strength North Korean force mounted an unsuccessful assault on the K Company roadblock on the Sukch'ŏn–P'yŏngyang road, sustaining five killed and seventeen taken prisoner.

At 10 a.m., Combat Cargo was over the drop zones for the second major drop of the operation. Forty C-119s dropped 220 tons of vehicles, rations, ammunition, water and 774 reinforcements. The reinforcements included Battery B, US 88th Anti-aircraft

American troop convoy advancing in North Korea. (Photo NARA)

Battalion, equipped with towed 40mm and M55 'quad fifty' weapons. The troops assembled on the drop zone and set up perimeter defences for the night.

Around mid-morning, two company combat teams moved south toward P'yŏngyang. While K Company had been tasked with conducting a 'reconnaissance in force' along the road, I Company had been ordered to execute the same mission, only along the railway line.

As I Company reached Op'a-ri at around 1 p.m., it was attacked by a battalion-strength North Korean force. Supported by 120mm mortars and 40mm guns, after a two-and-a-half-hour firefight, the enemy overran two I Company platoons.

With ninety men missing, the company was forced to pull back to high ground along Hill 281. However, the North Koreans failed to press home the advantage, electing instead

95

to retire to commanding positions around Op'a-ri and Sinopa. Twenty-nine members of I Company lost their lives in the attack, and ten bodies were never recovered. The remains of the rest were buried in a combat grave, in their parachutes, at the UN Cemetery in P'yŏngyang, on 26 October 1950. By December, the North Korean capital had been retaken by the enemy. However, the remains of these paratroopers were later disinterred and repatriated to the United States during Operation Glory and buried at Arlington National Cemetery in 1955.

MEDAL OF HONOR

Private First Class Richard Gene Wilson
Medical Company, 187th Airborne Regimental Combat Team
Attached to I Company

Pfc. Wilson distinguished himself by conspicuous gallantry and intrepidity above and beyond the call of duty in action.

As medical aid man attached to Company I, he accompanied the unit during a reconnaissance in force through the hilly country near Opari. The main body of the company was passing through a narrow valley flanked on 3 sides by high hills when the enemy laid down a barrage of mortar, automatic-weapons and small-arms fire. The company suffered a large number of casualties from the intense hostile fire while fighting its way out of the ambush.

Pfc. Wilson proceeded at once to move among the wounded and administered aid to them oblivious of the danger to himself, constantly exposing himself to hostile fire. The company commander ordered a withdrawal as the enemy threatened to encircle and isolate the company. As his unit withdrew Private Wilson assisted wounded men to safety and assured himself that none were left behind. After the company had pulled back, he learned that a comrade previously thought dead had been seen to be moving and attempting to crawl to safety. Despite the protests of his comrades, unarmed and facing a merciless enemy, Pfc. Wilson returned to the dangerous position in search of his comrade. Two days later a patrol found him lying beside the man he returned to aid. He had been shot several times while trying to shield and administer aid to the wounded man. Pfc. Wilson's superb personal bravery, consummate courage and willing self-sacrifice for his comrades reflect untold glory upon himself and uphold the esteemed traditions of the military service.[*]

---

[*] Medal of Honor Citations. United States Army Center of Military History.

Three miles away, the KPA 239th Regiment was positioned on a line of high hills that straddled both the road and railway on the Yongju–Op'a-ri axis, poised to escape northward under the cover of darkness. At around midnight, in the enemy's first assault on K Company's roadblock, a handful of North Koreans infiltrated the company command post, severely wounding the commander Captain Claude K. Josey with PPSh fire, before being killed or beaten off. A while later, now 22 October, the roadblock in the proximity of Hill 163 came under enemy attack, forcing the Americans to withdraw when they ran out of ammunition. Seizing the initiative, the North Koreans launched a third attack at 4 a.m., but unwittingly ran into the L Company perimeter and the 3/187th command post.

Despite sustaining heavy losses, the North Koreans launched a more determined attack: 300 men against L Company and 450 on Headquarters Company. At this point, the Americans radioed a desperate appeal for help—two men of HQ Company, three from L Company and a medic had already been killed. Two miles to the north, Brigadier Coad could hear the fierce firefight in the darkness.

The previous day, the 27th British was spearheading the US Eighth Army's advance north of P'yŏngyang on the road to Sukch'ŏn, with the objective of reaching the Ch'ŏngch'ŏn River. As he neared Yongju, Brigadier Coad halted for the night. It was here that he heard news of the plight of the airborne Americans just down the road north of Yongju.

As dawn broke the next morning, two companies of 1/Argylls entered and held Yongju. There, Captain A. P. Denness's C Company, 3RAR, led the battalion through the 1/Argylls, riding M-4 Sherman tanks of D Company, US 89th Tank Battalion, on attachment from the US Eighth Army. The artillery to the rear, however, had received strict orders not to use their guns because of the unknown exact locality of the American paratroopers.

Around 9 a.m., Captain Denness came under small-arms and mortar fire from an apple orchard a mile north of Yongju. Fifteen minutes later, with the Americans' position established as being between the 55 and 56 grid lines, the Australians launched their attack, under cover of fire from the Shermans. Lieutenant Townsend's 8 Platoon moved down the road before striking north, while 7 Platoon, commanded by Lieutenant Morison,

The Soviet-made PPSh-41, mainstay of Communist forces. (Photo Lposka)

attacked from the road. Lieutenant Butler's 9 Platoon remained close to the road to protect the attacking platoons' flanks.

At this point, 3RAR commanding officer, Colonel Charles Green, committed all his rifle companies to the attack and set up his headquarters in the apple orchard. He and his staff were immediately set on by a group of North Koreans, but in close-quarter combat in which thirty-four of their number were killed, the enemy was beaten off.

Colonel Green, in his typical concise manner, diarizes the events on that day:

> As there were a number of enemy in the vicinity of Tactical Headquarters, D Company was ordered to clear the area of YD 231538. When 7 and 8 Platoons had secured the spur at YD 2354 the tanks and 9 Platoon moved forward and contacted 503rd [sic] Airborne Battalion Headquarters at YD 241555.
>
> This battalion had been attacked at 0600 hours that morning and had suffered a number of casualties. Many enemy attempted to escape the ever-increasing gap between the Airborne and the battalion by fleeing across the open paddy fields to the west of the road. These, however, ran into tank fire and the fire of 9 Platoon.
>
> The battle was controlled throughout by wireless (No. 128), which operated satisfactorily. The enemy casualties were approximately 150 killed and 239 prisoners.*

3RAR was directed to remain in the orchard while 1/Argylls assembled at Yongju to the rear. 1/Middlesex now passed through the Australians and advanced on Sukch'ŏn, where they arrived at 3.30 p.m. and met up with the main force of the US 187th ARCT. From here, 1/Middlesex struck west to relieve a battalion of the 187th at Sinanju where they would then dig in for the night. Brigade HQ harboured for the night on the southern outskirts of Yongju, where North Koreans arrived in their droves, seeking warmth, shelter and food.

Early on 23 October, the US 2/187th marched across to Sukch'ŏn to join up with the US 3/187th, for trucking back to the vicinity of P'yŏngyang, departing at 5 p.m. The US 1/187th were withdrawn the following day.

Over three days of combat, the US 187th engaged around 6,000 North Koreans, killing almost 2,800 and capturing 3,000. In what became known as the Battle of Yongju, or the Battle of the Apple Orchard, American casualties amounted to forty-eight killed and eighty wounded in action, and one fatality and thirty-six injured in the drop. The Australians only suffered seven wounded.

The operation was deemed a success, especially in terms of strategic surprise. Many valuable lessons were learned for future airborne deployments, such as poor air-to-ground communications, inadequate training of transport loaders, and insufficient dropped trucks and jeeps for towing on the ground.

---

* 3rd Battalion, the Royal Australian Regiment War Diary, October 1950 (The Australia War Memorial Archives, Campbell).

LOGSTICS SUMMARY

Logistically, the air drops and aerial resupply of the 187th RCT were a success and provided the combat edge required for the 187th RCT to succeed in enemy territory until link-up with US Eighth Army forces. These operations were accomplished against an enemy whose lines of communication were short and who had the advantage of relying entirely on land LOCs.

The Sukchon-Sunchon Airdrop Operation, as the first combat air drop of troops since World War II and the first air drop of heavy equipment and heavy supply loads, became the base for developing the air drop doctrine and techniques plus procedures for future air drop operations.

The successful logistical support (air drop personnel, supplies and equipment) through air lines of communication opened a new era in U.S. military capability. This newly accepted capability included the use of helicopters for immediate evacuation of casualties, which reduced the mortality rate significantly, and the later use to resupply critical combat materiel. The importance of air drop logistics capabilities learned from Sukchon-Sunchon operations was evident by the successful resupply of the 1st (US) Marine Division and 7th (US) Infantry Division from 28 November 1950 through 9 December 1950. These units were trapped on the West and East sides of the Choshin Reservoir with land lines of communication resupply cut. Through aerial resupply these units of near Corps strength were sustained in combat for 12 days, against superior numbers of enemy until completion of a successful withdrawal. Based on the skills, experience, and training achieved during and after Sukchon-Sunchon, the same support units completed this largest air resupply operations in history by packaging and air dropping 1,643 tons and air landing 202 tons.[*]

---

[*] CSI Battlebook 4-C, *The Battle Of Sukchon-Sunchon* (Combat Studies Institute Fort Leavenworth, Kansas, 1984).

Ground objectives were largely met, except for one glaring failure. Ever since the Inch'ŏn amphibious landing and the US Eighth Army's breakout from the Pusan Perimeter, the liberation of United Nations PoWs remained high on the agenda. Whilst the North Koreans were directly responsible for the massacre of thousands of South Korean civilians, the ROKA military was not above perpetrating similar atrocities against North Koreans.

However, the discovery on 21 October of more than 130 bodies of murdered and maltreated American PoWs in a railway tunnel at Myŏnguch'am, north-west of Sunch'ŏn, sent shockwaves throughout the United States.

American PoWs in the hands of their North Korean captors, August 1950.

The US Senate Report No. 848 on Atrocities, dated 11 January 1954, records the proceedings of the hearing before the Senate Subcommittee on Korean War Atrocities, held on 2–4 December 1954. In a hearing whose purpose, described by sub-committee chairman Senator Charles E. Potter as being to bring

> the attention of the world in general and to the American people in particular the type of enemy the U.S. was fighting in Korea, to expose their horrible acts committed against our troops, and to foster appropriate legislation. The report concludes that the Communist armies were guilty of war crimes and crimes against humanity committed against American personnel from 1950 to 1953.[*]

Officially referring to the murder as 'The Sunchon Tunnel Massacre', the report states:

> In October of 1950, at Pyongyang, when the fall of that city appeared imminent, the Communists loaded approximately 180 American war prisoners into open railroad

---

[*] Permanent Subcommittee on Investigations of the Committee on Government Operations, United States Senate, Library of Congress (United States Government Printing Office, Washington, 1954).

A Stinson L-5 Sentinel. (Photo Captain Tom Greene)

cars for transport northward. These men were survivors of the Seoul-Pyongyang death march and were weak from lack of food, water, and medical care. They rode unprotected in the raw climate for 4 or 5 days, arriving at the Sunchon tunnel on October 30, 1950. Late in the afternoon, the prisoners were taken from the railroad cars in alternate groups of approximately 40 to nearby ravines, ostensibly to receive their first food in several days. There they were ruthlessly shot by North Korean soldiers, using Russian burp guns.

One hundred and thirty-eight American soldiers lost their lives in this atrocity; 68 were murdered at the tunnel, 7 died of malnutrition while in the tunnel, and the remainder died of pneumonia, dysentery, and malnutrition while in the tunnel, and the remainder died of pneumonia, dysentery, and malnutrition on the horror trip from Pyongyang.*

Task Force Rodgers, formed on the US 1/8th Cav and a company of tanks from the US 70th Tank Battalion, arrived at Sunch'ŏn on the morning of 21 October. Commanded by Lieutenant Colonel William M. Rodgers, the task force had been tasked to link up with the US 2/187th to augment its strength. Overhead, in a Stinson L-5 Sentinel liaison aircraft, commander of the US 1st Cavalry Division, General Hobart R. Gay and assistant division commander, Major General Frank A. Allen observed the junction of the two American units.

---

* Ibid.

Upon the latter's return to P'yŏngyang, he set off by road for Sunch'ŏn, accompanied by his aide and two American war correspondents. Shortly after arriving at the US 2/187th command post, General Allen received news of the murdered American PoWs in a tunnel 5 air miles north-west of the town. Allen set off immediately, stopping first at the ROKA 6th Infantry Division command post in Sunch'ŏn to get a South Korean colonel and an interpreter to accompany him in a second jeep.

Arriving at the tunnel just beyond Myŏnguch'am at 3 p.m., the party entered and discovered the corpses of seven emaciated American soldiers. Coming out at the northern end of the tunnel, Allen encountered ten live Americans who had hidden in scrub on both sides of the rail line. The survivors pointed out different spots where shot Americans would be found, some in shallow scrapes, others lying on the ground where they had been shot. Altogether, the bodies of seventy-two Americans were recovered. Of the twenty-three found alive, two succumbed that night.

In his evidence to the Senate atrocities sub-committee in December 1953, the seasoned General Allen declared:

> We found a very shallow grave, it must have contained at least 60 bodies, the other side of the road down maybe 50 yards from that place.
>
> It was beyond my comprehension that any human beings could treat other human beings as badly as our men were treated by the North Koreans. I could hardly believe that a human being could be so bestial as these people were.[*]

---

[*] Ibid.

6. RED INVASION

'Korea and our country are separated by a river. The safety of the Korean people has been threatened. It means that the safety of the Chinese people is also threatened.'

Professor Ch'ien Tuan-sheng, Dean, College of Social Studies,
Peking National University[*]

From the beginning of October 1950, the UN forces make-up became more international, resulting in US Eighth Army commander General Walton Walker establishing a United Nations Reception Centre (UNRC), under the aegis of the 2nd Logistical Command, on 8 October. Housed at the Taegu University, the facility served to acclimatize and kit out newly arrived UN troops.

Arriving first, the Thailand Battalion disembarked at Pusan on 3 October, followed by the main Thai contingent four days later, bringing the force to 4,000 ground troops. Commanded by the Thai crown prince Major General Prince Pisit Dispongsa-Diskul, the Thai expeditionary force was attached to the US 2nd Infantry Division. From 12 to 18 October, the 5,190-strong Turkish Brigade, commanded by General Tashin Yazici, was the next to arrive at Pusan. On 24 October, the British 28th Brigade and an advance party from the Netherlands Battalion landed in Korea.

As the United Nations airborne offensive against elements of a fleeing North Korean army entered its second day on 21 October, the North Korean government announced by radio that it had moved its capital from P'yŏngyang to Sinŭiju, one mile south of the Yalu River, on the Manchurian border, in the extreme north-west Korea. The announcement, made by a broadcasting station in Sinŭiju, cleared up the mystery of the whereabouts of North Korean leader Kim Il-sung and his inner circle of ministers and advisors.

Early in 1950, the US FEAF had conducted bombing missions on the two railway bridges that spanned the Yalu River connecting Sinŭiju with the Manchurian city of Antung (Dandong). The cross-border link represented a major supply route of troops and war matériel for the North Koreans. Communist China responded immediately by establishing an air base at Antung and stationing Mikoyan-Gurevich MiG-15 (NATO 'Fagot') fighter jets there.

However, this proved to be a transient move for the North Korean seat of power. The natural defences provided by the rugged, heavily wooded mountains of central North Korea was deemed more suitable and the town of Kanggye chosen as the new provisional capital and national military headquarters.

---

[*]   Chinese Communist broadcast, 14 October 1950.

The contingent of volunteers from the Netherlands arrives in Korea, October 1950. (Photo Anefo)

U.S. AID SOUGHT

'Full Scale War' In Indo-China

France wants more American arms, and quickly, for Indo-China, because she now 'has a full-scale war on her hands. The guerrilla phase is over,' a French Government spokesman said yesterday. French Prime Minister Pleven has instructed his Defence Minister, M. Moch, who is in Washington for defence talks, to make this request. The problem has been given urgency by French reverses in Indo-China, where Vietminh (Communist Insurgent) forces overwhelmed two retiring French forces in a reported slaughter of nearly 3,500 men. The spokesman said tanks, 'planes and parachutists' equipment were most urgently needed. Two more front-line combat divisions should be available in addition to the 110,000 strong French and Foreign Legion army.

NEW DEFENCE LINE

French Army H.Q. in Saigon announced yesterday that French and Vietnamese troops had established a new defence line after pulling out of Thai-Nguyen, the rebel capital. The withdrawal had not been made under guerrilla pressure a spokesman said. The new line is ten miles farther south, and 30 miles north of Hanoi, capital of the North Tonkin delta. Further French withdrawals from outposts near the Chinese frontier were expected.—Reuter.

Irish Independent, 13 October 1950

While the US 187th ARTC set about entrapping remnants of the KPA 239th Infantry Regiment along the Sukch'ŏn– Sunch'ŏn axis north of UN-occupied P'yŏngyang, US Eighth Army intelligence personnel were assessing North Korean defence capabilities of the Ch'ŏngch'ŏn River barrier, stretching from the Yalu River mouth near Sinanju and Anju, north-east to Hŭich'ŏn.

Predictions were made that there would be only nominal resistance, as the North Koreans would continue to flee ever northward along two principal road and rail routes. To the left, the coastal route doglegged west just before Pakch'ŏn, before terminating at Sinŭiju. The other route ran north-east from Anju along the Ch'ŏngch'ŏn River, passed through Hŭich'ŏn, and on to Kanggye 2 air miles from the Yalu.

On 22 October, C Company, 6th Medium Tank Battalion, titled Task Force Elephant, jumped off from P'yŏngyang for Kujang-dong, via Sunch'ŏn, to guard the rail line and keep the enemy away from that section of the Ch'ŏngch'ŏn. Equipped with M45 and M46 tanks, the task force arrived at its objective around 10 p.m., before following the river 20 miles downstream to Kunu-ri (also known as Keach'ŏn). The battalion was followed by the ROKA 1st Infantry Division, commanded by General Paik Sun-yup, who recovered forty escaped American PoWs en route. Two more escapees arrived at Kunu-ri the next morning.

Bridge over the Yalu River.

At 10 a.m. on the morning of 23 October, 1/Argylls led the 27th British convoy of US Army transport from Yongju, arriving at Sinanju—via Sukch'ŏn—at the demolished bridge over the Ch'ŏngch'ŏn. The advance had been uneventful until the brigade arrived at the south bank at 1 p.m. when the North Koreans opened up with artillery and small-arms fire from the north bank. 3RAR occupied high ground overlooking the river crossing a mile south-west of Sinanju, while 1/Middlesex commenced preparations to cross the river in assault boats the next day. 1/Argylls dug in on commanding ground above the bridge.

General Paik continued his downstream advance, knocking out two T-34 tanks and two self-propelled guns and capturing a serviceable T-34. Around noon, led by D Company tanks, Paik secured the damaged wooden bridge across the Ch'ŏngch'ŏn three miles before Anju. Division engineers commenced work on repairing the bridge in anticipation of a crossing the following morning. On 23–24 October, Paik successfully moved his three regiments over the bridge before attacking north-east along the road to Unsan.

By the end of 22 October, forward elements of the US 24th Infantry Division had started to arrive in its designated assembly area north of the North Korean capital. Division commander Major General John H. Church, in pursuance of US I Corps orders, assumed control of the 27th British, the US 89th Medium Tank Battalion and the US 90th FAB.

At the Sinanju crossing point, the Ch'ŏngch'ŏn River was subjected to a 22-foot tidal-rise and-fall range. At low tide, deep mud banks would make the launching of boats along the river's edge impossible. Having gleaned from local villagers that high tide would be at 7 a.m. the next morning, Brigadier Coad issued orders for 1/Middlesex to be ready to cross at that time. Tactically, 1/Middlesex, upon beaching on the north bank, was to advance on a flanking attack to secure high ground overlooking the hamlet of Maengjang-dong. 3RAR would be on alert too if required, to pass through 1/Middlesex to secure the objective.

Shortly after sunset, American engineers delivered thirty assault boats. At the same time, they conducted a reconnaissance of the bridge to assess what was needed to make the road bridge usable to heavy traffic. For the rest of the day, a steady stream of enemy soldiers surrendered to UN forces. Unable to find their parent units in the confusion of retreat, and finding themselves helplessly trapped on the south bank, the North Koreans willingly gave themselves up in large numbers.

On the morning of 24 October, 1/Middlesex crossing was delayed until 8.30 a.m. The 27th British diary entry for the day recorded the operation:

> The crossing of the CHONGCHON RIVER was delayed till 0830hrs this morning as high tide flowed later than expected. Even so, when 1 MX [Middlesex] did cross a coy [company] at a time, the flow of water was fast enough to drift the assault boats well

Two boys serving with the North Korean army taken prisoner. (Photo NARA)

off their course and, by the time they had returned for the second lift, they were well upstream from their starting point.

The crossing this morning was probably unique amongst assault crossings for, as the leading troops started out, crowds of villagers gathered on the far bank cheering and waving flags. Nor was this all, for on seeing the difficulties our soldiers had in controlling their craft, for no engineer assistance was available as boatmasters, several fishing boats put out from the far bank to help them over!

On successfully crossing the river, 1/Middlesex advanced to the north-east on their objective at Maengjang-dong, in the vicinity of Hill 93. 3RAR was stood down as they were not required to assist the Middlesex battalion. The Australians welcomed their first issue of US Army clothing: field jackets.

At this time, General MacArthur issued fresh orders to all his ground commanders, rescinding previous related orders and lifting all restrictions on UNC deployments south of the Yalu River border. On 24 October, a signal from the JCS in Washington challenged

MacArthur's radical deviation from the directive of 27 September. MacArthur had no problem justifying his decision, contending that military necessity, based on the inability of the South Koreans to sustain the offensive on their own, had forced his hand in the manner in which he had to prosecute the war. He also deemed it fit to remind his military superiors that the whole issue had been dealt with when he met with President Truman on Wake Island.

To the right of the US I Corps, two divisions of the ROKA II Corps had also joined the UN advance, moving into extremely mountainous terrain. On the South Korean left flank, the ROKA 6th Infantry Division had turned north-east at Kunu-ri and was moving along the road on the south bank of the Ch'ŏngch'ŏn that led to Hŭich'ŏn, and from there to Kanggye. To the right, the ROKA 8th Infantry Division had arrived at Tŏkch'ŏn late on the night of 23 October, from where it struck north to reach Kujang-dong two days later.

As the ROKA 6th Infantry Division advanced between Kunu-ri and Kujang-dong, the South Koreans seized two North Korean trains, capturing eight tanks and a large haul of ammunition. As the division advanced farther, they engaged elements of the KPA 25th Regiment in heavy combat before the North Koreans scattered. Entering Hŭich'ŏn on the night of 23 October, the South Koreans captured another twenty T-34 tanks. From here, the division jumped off for Ch'osan on the Yalu River border with Manchuria as its objective, and in doing so was outstripping the rest of the UN forces.

Having crossed the Ch'ŏngch'ŏn, Brigadier Coad now faced the major problem of getting his tanks and vehicles to the north bank. The damaged bridges would not sustain the weight and the engineers did not have sufficient appropriate material to repair the structures. A pontoon foot bridge could not be rigged up either. Coad was essentially left with only two options: locate another bridge or establish a ferry crossing. The latter, however, proved unworkable as the cyclical tidal ebb and flow of the river, running at around eight knots, would only allow three hours of slack water in every twenty-four in which to use a ferry. Finally, Coad was given division HQ permission to cross on the bridge near Anju in the ROKA 1st Infantry Division sector. The bridge would not take the weight of the armour, but it was planned for the next day—25 October—to get the 1/Middlesex transport over to the north bank, followed by the rest of the brigade.

During the day, a 1/Argylls reconnaissance patrol was despatched to Anju, where they found that the town was safely in South Korean hands. 3RAR, meanwhile, spent the day preparing to lead the brigade jump-off in the morning. Colonel Green fixed the battalion's order of march, placing B Company, commanded by Major N. Thirwell MC, in the front. D Company, US 89th Tank Battalion, was to accompany Thirwell. Tactical HQ would follow, and behind them A Company, under Major R. A. Gordon, C Company under Captain A. Denness, with Major W. F. Brown's D Company bringing up the rear.

At 10 a.m., 3RAR trucked out from Sinanju, crossing the Ch'ŏngch'ŏn at Anju ninety minutes later. The battalion then harboured 3 miles north-west of Anju to wait for

A US Navy Douglas AD-3 Skyraider drops its payload on bridges over the Yalu River. (Photo US Navy)

the tanks. At 2 p.m., the decision was made to carry on without the tanks that were encountering problems in getting across the river. Two hours later B Company arrived at the village of Kujin, a mile south of Pakch'ŏn. Here, the main road to Sinuiju, via Ch'ongju, branched off to the west, crossing the Taeryong River. The concrete bridge spanning the river had been demolished, but two sections of 4 Platoon, B Company, led by Lieutenant A. L. Morrison, were able to clamber over the broken span on to the west bank. To Morrison's right, around fifty unarmed North Korean soldiers, their hands in the air, now approached from high ground. As they neared the Australians, concealed enemy troops opened up heavy but inaccurate small-arms fire from the high ground.

Overhead, the support Mosquito aircraft reported having sighted two enemy companies close to Morrison's position. The Australians were withdrawn straight away, taking with them ten enemy prisoners. At 5.15 p.m., directed by the Mosquito airborne controller, F-80 Shooting Star fighters strafed the ridges to the immediate west of the Taeryong. As the jets broke off, artillery and 3-inch mortar fire took over the softening process.

RED ADVISERS IN NORTH KOREAN ARMY

A Central News Agency reporter from the Korean war front reported that he learned from a number of North Korean POWs who spoke fluent Chinese that Russian advisers are now holding important command positions in the North Korean Army and that they are actively participating in the war.

The reporter stated that he obtained the following additional information from the PoWs in his interviews:

1. In early 1950, the units of the CCF Fourth Field Army in the Northeast were ordered to cross the Yalu River.
2. The units that these prisoners of war were assigned to were formerly stationed in the Northeast, and they were ordered to cross the Yalu River on 18 April 1950.
3. The POWs were assigned to the CCF in 1945 and have actively participated in the Chinese civil war.
4. Many CCF-trained North Koreans were sent to a guerrilla school located somewhere in North Korea for one month and later infiltrated the eastern coast of South Korea to carry out guerrilla activities.
5. The POWs heard rumors that Chinese Communist troops are now participating in the Korean war but that they have never seen them.

It is also reported that a captured first lieutenant of the North Korean Army stated that three Russian advisers are now attached to each North Korean regiment.[*]

---

[*] CIA Information from Foreign Documents or Radio Broadcasts 'Russians Active in Korean War', 11 August 1950.

At Pakch'ŏn, D Company, 3RAR, completed a clearing exercise, returning with 225 North Korean prisoners. A platoon from D Company and a platoon of engineers from the US 72nd Engineer Combat Battalion remained behind to provide rearguard cover while a ford was erected across the river. By 7 p.m. all four 3RAR combat companies, less the D Company platoon, had crossed over to the west bank for the night. B Company dug in on the right of the road and A Company on the left, while C and D companies and the tanks protected the rear on the south bank. However, there would be no time for the Australians to rest.

To the west of their bivouac, at 7.30 p.m. elements the enemy commenced a night of sporadic harassment. B Company 3-inch mortars discouraged assembling enemy soldiers from launching a frontal assault. Thirty minutes later North Korean shells, thought to be armour-piercing from a self-propelled gun, landed in the C Company and battalion command post areas, but failed to explode.

Around 10.30 p.m., A and B companies in their forward positions faced an increase in enemy activity. A short while later, 8 Platoon, C Company was brought forward to reinforce A Company. The two companies supported by artillery and mortar fire, repelled groups of North Koreans attacking their positions. B Company suffered two killed and three wounded. A lull in enemy activity ensued for the next few hours into 26 October.

At around 4 a.m., a North Korean colonel in a jeep led a tank and sixty infantry on to B Company's position. A second T-34, a distance

Lieutenant-Colonel Charles Green, commanding officer, 3RAR. (Photo AWM)

to the enemy's rear, fired its turret gun at the Australians. The occupants of the jeep were quickly taken care of, but the accompanying tank drove right up to B Company HQ, firing and killing a member of the US 90th FAB forward observation party. The B Company 3.5-inch bazooka operator failed to get a shot off, which, according to battalion records was due to human error as the operator failed to release the safety catch in the 'excitement of the moment'. Brigade, however, recorded that the weapon's electric firing mechanism had been faulty.

The tank fired its way through A and B companies and came to within 100 yards of the bridge before realizing that he was on his own. It promptly reversed all the way back through the Australians, firing erratically. At this, the rest of the North Koreans broke off and fell back, abandoning two Soviet-type jeeps and a motorcycle, and leaving their colonel's body behind. They did not return. At 7 a.m., three airstrikes hit the North Korean positions on the ridges to the west of A and B companies.

Maps and documents recovered from the dead North Korean colonel yielded valuable intelligence on enemy defensive positions west of the Taeryong River. The maps showed the KPA 17th Tank Brigade, equipped with twenty tanks and six artillery pieces in support, positioned along the Pakch'ŏn–Ch'ongju road. It was discovered that the North Korean officer was a senior Culture and Propaganda officer on attachment to the tank brigade.

At 11 a.m. that morning, D Company, 3RAR, and the tanks crossed the Taeryong River at Pakch'ŏn, leaving only battalion HQ and Support Company east of the river. Colonel Green estimated that more than 100 North Koreans had been killed, while 38 were taken prisoner. It had also been a costly night for his battalion, with eight killed and twenty-two wounded. The dead were buried in a Christian cemetery in Pakch'ŏn.

For the remainder of the day, 1/Middlesex and 1/Argylls crossed the river and continued to advance toward Ch'ongju, without encountering any North Koreans. That night, engineers completed repairs to the bridge and the remaining brigade echelon units and tanks joined the rest of the brigade west of the river. The brigade, including brigade HQ, harboured at Pakch'ŏn for the night.

By 11 a.m. the following morning—27 October—the whole brigade had crossed the Taeryong and had started their advance on Taech'ŏn directly to the north. From this point, the brigade was to face a significant increase in North Korean resistance.

Having neutralized two enemy tanks with the support of an airstrike, as the leading 1/Middlesex was passing through Yŏngsŏng-ni, the battalion was met with such

A Bell H-13 Sioux helicopter of a US Mobile Army Surgical Hospital (MASH), US Eighth Army. (Photo Sergeant Paul E. Norman)

heavy North Korean small-arms, artillery and tank fire, that it was forced to withdraw to regroup. Launching a 'set-piece battalion' counterattack, bitter fighting ensued as the British troops gradually took the hills to the west of the village. During the prolonged day's action, ten North Korean tanks and two self-propelled guns were destroyed, with the enemy suffering seventy-five casualties and twenty taken prisoner. The 1/Middlesex lost three killed and four wounded.

That night, cognizant of the fact that 'the days of swift advance' were over, Brigadier Coad adapted his tactics to that of a more deliberate advance, immediately implementing 'advance-to-contact' techniques.

At 8 a.m. the next morning, a tank-mounted platoon from the 1/Argylls set off first as an advance guard, followed several hundred yards behind by the rest of the company. The main battalion force then followed less than a mile to the rear. The manoeuvre ensured that Coad's axis of advance was kept clear of enemy troops. As it transpired, there were only a few minor skirmishes in and around Napch'ŏngjŏng, before the brigade

---

POW REPORTS OF CHINESE COMMUNIST FORCES IN NORTH KOREA

The Commanding General of the US Eighth Army in Korea reports that the ten Chinese Communist prisoners of war captured as of 30 October have claimed during interrogations that the 119th and 120th divisions of the Chinese 40th Army and the 117th division of the 39th Army are now in Korea.

CIA Comment
Although there are major units of Chinese Communist forces along the Manchurian–Korean border, the presence of Chinese Communist units in Korea has not been confirmed. CIA continues to believe that direct Chinese Communist intervention in Korea is unlikely at this time. However, there is a strong possibility that the Peiping regime may move troops across the border in an effort to establish a 'cordon sanitaire' around the Suiho hydroelectric plant and other strategic border installations essential to the Manchurian economy.

There is also the possibility that these Chinese were sent into North Korea to plant reports of Chinese of Chinese Communist forces in North Korea in the hope of slowing the UN advance, and thereby providing time for North Korean forces to reorganize. Ordinarily, privates in the Chinese army do not possess the detailed order-of-battle information which these POWs passed on to US field interrogators.[*]

---

[*] CIA Daily Summary, October 1950 to December 1950.

harboured for the night: 1/Argylls on both sides of the road, 3RAR and brigade HQ a mile short of the Scots, and 1/Middlesex guarding a crossroads junction.

On 29 October, 3RAR passed through 1/Argylls, almost immediately encountering heavy enemy tank, self-propelled gun and small-arms fire from high ground to the south of the road. After an airstrike, which disabled four T-34s, the Australians launched an artillery- and mortar-led attack on the well-entrenched enemy position on the left. Eventually seizing the hill and repelling a concerted enemy counterattack, the battalion turned its attention on the high ground to the north of the road. Here, too, the North Koreans put up a determined defence before finally evacuating their position. By 9 p.m. that night, the enemy had broken off repeated attempts at retaking the high ground.

The next day, Brigadier Coad attended an operations meeting at the US 24th Infantry Division HQ, where he received instructions to seize and hold Ch'ongju, to allow the US 21st RCT safe passage through the town on its way to the Yalu River. The British and Australian battalions met only light resistance, and at 5.15 p.m., the 1/Argylls declared the town free of enemy troops.

At this juncture, the Australians suffered a major blow. With Ch'ongju secure, another battalion took point to allow 3RAR to find somewhere to rest for the afternoon. Battalion commander, 30-year-old Lieutenant-Colonel Charles H. Green DSO, had been resting in his pup tent near his men when Chinese artillery dropped six high-velocity shells in the area. Colonel Green sustained the only injury, with severe shrapnel wounds to the stomach. On 1 November, the much-admired and respected commander succumbed to his wounds at Sinanju. He is buried in the UN War Cemetery in Pusan. The United States posthumously awarded Colonel Green the Silver Star Medal.

Battalion intelligence officer, Lieutenant A. Argent, described his erstwhile commander as

a tall, dark, sinewy man with the bearing, and unhurried deliberateness one usually associates with men of the land. Pressure never seemed to bother him. He had a fine touch and the presence of a natural leader. His command in Korea was always firm and sure. He always gave good, clear and concise orders. He kept well forward, in fact immediately behind the leading company group. After six weeks he had moulded the battalion into a fighting unit.[*]

For the first time since entering the Korean theatre, the 27th British had a day of rest at Ch'ongju on 31 October.

Meanwhile, to the east, in the ROKA II Corps sector, the 7th Regiment, ROKA 6th Infantry Division, had left the Ch'ŏngch'ŏn valley and passed through Onjŏng. Late on the afternoon of 25 October, the regiment entered the town of Kojang, now only 18 air miles south of Ch'osan and the Manchurian border, and bivouacked there for the night.

---

[*]   The Australian War Memorial at www.awm.gov.au/.

The next morning—26 October—the American KMAG advisor with the ROKA 7th Regiment, Major Harry Fleming joined a reconnaissance sortie into Ch'osan. Upon observing fleeing North Korean troops crossing the Yalu River on a narrow footbridge, the South Koreans directed machine-gun fire at the retreating enemy, ensuring that no fire landed in China. After securing the town, the next day the rest of the regiment moved in, becoming the first UN unit to reach the Chinese border, and, as the war turned once more, it would be the only unit under US Eighth Army command to reach the border during the conflict.

On 25 October, the complexion of the Korean War changed irrevocably with a dramatic shift in the balance of power on the peninsula.

By this time, the ROKA 6th Infantry Division, under Colonel Park Kwang Hyuk, had reached the Unsan–Onjŏng axis on its northward advance. From the village of Onjŏng, the ROKA 2nd Regiment struck north-west toward Pukchin with Pyŏktong on the Yalu River as its objective.

Eight miles out of Onjŏng, the regiment's leading 3rd Battalion drove into a Chinese People's Volunteer Army (CPVA) ambush in which the South Korean battalion ceased to exist as an organized military entity. At first believing it to be a North Korean trap, the South Koreans had in fact encountered the CPVA XL Corps, commanded by Wen Yuchen, comprising the 118th, 119th and 120th divisions, each with a strength of 10,000.

Troops of the Chinese People's Volunteer Army, 1950.

About half of the South Korean battalion managed to escape, returning to Onjŏng in splintered groups later in the afternoon. The battalion's KMAG advisor, Lieutenant Glen C. Jones was taken prisoner. He would die in captivity.

As early as 13 July 1950, under direct orders from Communist Chinese leader Mao Zedong, the Central Military Commission in Beijing had activated the Northeast Border Defence Army. Initially comprising the Twenty-ninth, Thirty-eighth, Fortieth and Forty-second field armies, with artillery and air defence capabilities, by the end of July 225,000 Chinese troops were in position along the border with North Korea.

Despite his close relationship with ally and sponsor the Soviet Union, at the end of September, and while Beijing continued to mass its forces in Manchuria, North Korean leader Kim Il-sung made a formal request for Chinese military assistance. Archival documents suggest that at the beginning of October, Mao acknowledged the inevitability and necessity of war. On 8 October, he issued a directive for the Northeast Border Defence Army to be retitled the 'Chinese People's Volunteers', a seemingly transparent mechanism for China to go to war with the US and her Korean War allies. Mao looked to Marshal Peng Dehuai, veteran of the Communist struggle against the Nationalist Chinese and the Japanese, to command the force.

As large numbers of Chinese troops quietly started to infiltrate North Korea on 12 October, the CIA in Washington informed President Truman that

the Chinese Communist ground forces, currently lacking requisite air and naval support, are capable of intervening, but not necessarily decisively, in the Korean conflict. There are no convincing indications of an actual Chinese Communist intention to resort to full-scale intervention in Korea.

After reviewing the factors favoring, and those opposing, Chinese Communist intervention, it is concluded that while full-scale Chinese Communist intervention in Korea must be regarded as a continuing possibility, a consideration of all known factors leads to the conclusion that barring a Soviet decision for global war, such action is not probable in 1950. During this period, intervention will probably be confined to continued covert assistance to the North Koreans.[*]

Not for the first time since the start of 1950, American intelligence failed to adequately assess the situation and potential threats in the sub-region.

At 3.30 a.m. on 26 October, the Chinese launched an attack on the ROKA 2nd Regiment in Onjŏng, causing widespread panic among the South Koreans. At 6 a.m., elements of the CPVA XL Corps breeched the South Koreans' defences, forcing them to withdraw to the east. Three miles down the road, they ran into a

---

[*] *Study of CIA Reporting on Chinese Communist Intervention in the Korean War, September–December 1950* (CIA Historical Staff, 17 October 1955).

Chinese roadblock, precipitating a mass bombshelling without posing any meaningful challenge to the CPVA troops. This lack of resistance by the South Koreans was confirmed when more than 2,700 soldiers out of a regimental strength of 3,100 arrived back at the Ch'ŏngch'ŏn River.

At this time, the ROKA 19th Regiment, less one battalion, and the 10th Regiment, ROKA 8th Infantry Division, were in Hŭich'ŏn. Commander of the ROKA II Corps, Major General Yu, ordered both regiments, less 1st Battalion, ROKA 10th Regiment, to hold the town, to jump off to the west to recover the abandoned ROKA 2nd Regiment vehicles and artillery pieces. However, these South Korean units were also defeated by the Chinese, losing their vehicles and all three artillery batteries.

Fearing that the cut-off ROKA 7th Regiment would meet the same fate, ROKA 6th Infantry Division HQ ordered the regiment to immediately fall back on the division. By this time, though, the ROKA 7th Regiment was desperate for a resupply of fuel, food and ammunition, without which they could not move. It would be two days before the airdrop took place, and on the morning of 29 October, the regiment started to withdraw to the south.

When we look at the war in Korea it's disturbing. But I also think that we can't stop being wary of what the USSR is doing elsewhere in the world as well.

The Foreign Secretary said yesterday that he didn't know whether the Russians and Chinese were planning a Communist takeover of the world. But he thought that there was no danger of an attack by Russia in Europe while war went on in Korea.

I disagree. I think that this could be a plan to get the US and the UN to commit forces to China and weaken our forces here in Europe. For this reason I hoped that General MacArthur's advance would stop and leave a no-man's land. I'm not sure now whether this will happen.

I'm sure that all MPs agree that the sooner we can establish a settlement in the Far East the better. For it's in Europe that the Cold War will be won or lost. We also shouldn't criticise the US or their commanders or do anything to upset the Americans. We fight together under the banner of the United Nations but they're taking on most of the burden.

The Americans have suffered much higher casualties than we have. This shows their commitment. Our own troops are brave and we worry about them. But our presence in Korea is mostly a symbol of our loyalty to the US.

Winston Churchill, 'The International Situation' speech to the House of Commons

30 November 1950

Twenty miles south of Kojang a battalion from the 373rd Regiment, CPVA 125th Infantry Division, was waiting for the South Koreans. The whole regiment was committed to the ensuing firefight as the tactical air control party called in an airstrike. As night

An American Sikorsky YH-19 on a resupply drop. (Photo USAF)

The wreckage of a bridge and a North Korean tank south of Suwon. The tank was caught on a bridge and put out of action by air strikes, 7 October 1951. (US Army)

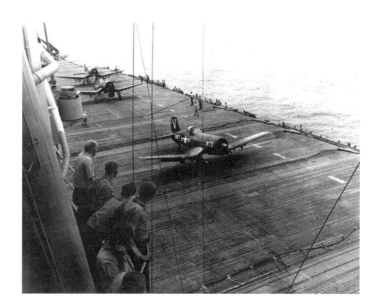

Vought F4U-4B Corsair fighters taking off from the aircraft carrier USS *Philippine Sea*, October 1950. (Photo US Navy)

Yongju area, North Korea, 22 October 1950. Covered by a greatcoat, a North Korean soldier lies on a stretcher and awaits medical evacuation after he has been wounded in the Battle of the Apple Orchard by members of the 3rd Battalion, The Royal Australian Regiment (3RAR). Standing with an Owen gun slung over his shoulder, Corporal Mick Hatton (left) casually rests his foot on one of the stretcher's handles. At rear, with a cigarette dangling from his mouth, Sergeant Ian Robertson, an official photographer and member of the Sniper Section, reaches into a bag he has hanging on his shoulder. (Photo Australian War Memorial)

fell, any semblance of resistance evaporated as most of the South Koreans fled into the surrounding hills. Wounded in fifteen places, KMAG officer Major Harry Fleming was the only American to survive. He was taken prisoner and would spend the next three years incarcerated in a Chinese prison camp. Of the 3,500 men of the ROKA 7th Regiment, only 875, including commanding officer Colonel Lim Bu Taik, reached the division at Kunu-ri.

With the collapse of the ROKA II Corps on the US Eighth Army's right, General Walker released the ROKA 7th Infantry Division from US I Corps' command, to return to the ROKA II Corps. The ROKA 8th Infantry Division then took up a defensive line north of the Ch'ŏngch'ŏn River on the Yŏngbyŏn*–Kujang-dong axis, and from there the ROKA 7th Infantry Division would extend the line south to Tokch'on.

On 31 October, the Chinese breeched the ROKA II Corps defensive line when they broke through the 16th Regiment, ROKA 8th Infantry Division, on the boundary of the ROKA 1st Infantry Division sector. The ROKA II Corps then turned more to the east in an attempt to stem the onslaught of Chinese forces. This created a vulnerable gap between the South Koreans' left flank and the right of the US Eighth Army. General Walker immediately concentrated the US 2nd Infantry Division in the Sunch'ŏn area.

By 1 November, the Chinese had effectively disabled the ROKA II Corps, and had moved on to General Walker's open right flank south of the Ch'ŏngch'ŏn. To his front, the unstoppable communist forces also threatened the centre of the US Eighth Army at Unsan.

Six Chinese infantry corps, comprising 18 divisions, and 3 artillery divisions, estimated at between 250,000 and 400,000 men, had arrived in front of General MacArthur's UN forces. Not only did this put an abrupt end to the general's boasts of a quick victory and an early end to the war, but also threatened to bring about a shocking and bloody reversal of fortunes. MacArthur was only months away from being dismissed by President Truman.

---

* Today, Yŏngbyŏn is North Korea's major nuclear facility, operating the country's first nuclear reactors. In 2018, in an agreement with South Korea, the North Korean government asserted that it would only dismantle Yŏngbyŏn if the US engaged in like reciprocal action.

SOURCES

My sincere thanks, as always, to the unflagging support I receive from Colonel Dudley Wall. His drawings of maps and military equipment and images of militaria from his private expansive collection never fail to enrich my work.

24th US Division War Diary, September–October 1950. (Adjutant General's Office, Department of the Army, Washington)

27th British Commonwealth Brigade War Diary, September to October 1950. (The Australia War Memorial archives, Campbell)

3rd Battalion, the Royal Australian War Diary, October 1950. (The Australia War Memorial archives, Campbell)

Appleman, Roy E., 'South to the Naktong, North to the Yalu (June–November 1950)', *United States in the Korean War.* (Center Of Military History, United States Army, Washington, D.C., 1992)

Blanton, Stephen Dwight, *A Study of the United States Navy's Minesweeping Efforts in the Korean War*, Texas Tech University, August 1993.

Boose, Donald W. Jnr, *US Army Forces in the Korean War.* (Osprey Publishing, Oxford, 2005)

Central Intelligence Agency (CIA) declassified documents.

Cunningham-Boothe, Ashley and Farrar, Peter (Eds.), *British Forces in the Korean War.* (The British Korean Veterans Association, Halifax, 1988)

Daily, Edward L., *Strike Swiftly Korea: 70th Heavy Tank Battalion, 1950–1953* (Turner Publishing Company, Nashville, 1988)

Fehrenbach, T.R., *This Kind of War: The Classic Korean War History* (Potomac Books, 2000)

Futrell, Robert Frank, *The United States Air Force in Korea, 1950–1953* (Progressive Management, 1983)

Gugeler, Russell A., *Combat Actions in Korea* (Center of Military History United States Army, Washington D.C., 1954).

Hastings, Max, *The Korean War* (Pan, London, 1987).

Korean War Project, www.koreanwar.org/

Knox, Donald, *The Korean War, Pusan to Chosin: An Oral History.* (Harcourt Brace & Co., Orlando, 1985)

McElroy, Paul, United States Naval Reserve, *The Mining of Wonsan Harbor, North Korea in 1950: Lessons for Today's Navy.* (1999)

Pittman, Maj (P) Phill, et al, *The Battle Of Sukchon-Sunchon 20 - 25 October, 1950.* (Combat Studies Institute, Fort Leavenworth, May 1984)

Sloan, Bill, *The Darkest Summer; Pusan and Inch'ŏn 1950* (Simon and Schuster Paperbacks, New York, 2009).

Tucker, Spencer C., Ed., *Encyclopedia of the Korean War* (Checkmark Books, New York, 2002).

United States Army Records, National Archives and Records Administration (NARA), College Park, Maryland, USA.

van Tonder, Gerry, *North Korea Invades the South: Across the 38th Parallel, June 1950.* (Pen and Sword Military, Barnsley, 2018)

van Tonder, Gerry, *North Korean Onslaught: UN Stand at the Pusan Perimeter, August–September 1950.* (Pen and Sword Military, Barnsley, 2018)

van Tonder, Gerry, *Korean War, Inch'ŏn Landing: MacArthur's Masterstroke, September 1950* (Pen and Sword Military, Barnsley, 2019)

War Diary X Corps Monthly Summary 1 Oct 1950 to 31 Oct 1950.

A Marine guards KPA prisoners on a board a US warship. (Photo US Navy)

Index

About the Author

Born in Southern Rhodesia, now Zimbabwe, historian and author Gerry van Tonder came to Britain in 1999. Specializing in military history, Gerry started his writing career with titles about twentieth-century guerrilla and open warfare in southern Africa, including the co-authored definitive *Rhodesia Regiment 1899–1981*. Gerry presented a copy of this title to the regiment's former colonel-in-chief, Her Majesty the Queen. Having written over twenty books, Gerry writes extensively for several Pen & Sword military history series including 'Cold War 1945–1991', 'Military Legacy' (focusing on the heritage of British cities), 'Echoes of the Blitz', and 'History of Terror'.

Other titles by Gerry van Tonder

Inch'ŏn Landing: MacArthur's Korean War Masterstroke, September 1950

North Korean Onslaught: UN Stand at the Pusan Perimeter August–September 1950

SS Einsatzgruppen: Nazi Death Squads 1939–1945

Irgun: Revisionist Zionism 1931–1948

Sino-Indian War: October–November 1962

Echoes of the Coventry Blitz

Red China: Mao Crushes Chiang's Kuomintang, 1949

North Korea Invades the South: Across the 38th Parallel, June 1950

Berlin Blockade: Soviet Chokehold and the Great Allied Airlift 1948–1949

Malayan Emergency: Triumph of the Running Dogs 1948–1960

Nottingham's Military Legacy

Sheffield's Military Legacy

Derby in 50 Buildings

Chesterfield's Military Heritage

Mansfield Through Time

Rhodesian African Rifles/Rhodesia Native Regiment Book of Remembrance

Lt-Gen Keith Coster: A Life in Uniform

Rhodesian Combined Forces Roll of Honour 1966-1981

Rhodesia Regiment 1899–1981

Operation Lighthouse: Intaf in the Rhodesian Bush War 1972–1980

North of the Red Line: Recollections of the Border War by Members of the South African Armed Forces: 1966–1989